Manifesto

A Blueprint for
Missional Church

NIC HARDING

RIVER
PUBLISHING

River Publishing & Media Ltd
Barham Court
Teston
Maidstone
Kent
ME18 5BZ
United Kingdom

info@river-publishing.co.uk

ISBN 978-1-908393-17-3

Printed in the United Kingdom

Contents

What people have said...

Nic Harding is a doctor by profession. He is also a pastor who now leads one of the most remarkable churches in the country. In this book he unfolds his vision, his wisdom and his heart It is full of practical guidance on how to build a church that will have impact and influence in the community.

Nicky Gumbel – Vicar of Holy Trinity Brompton and the pioneer of the Alpha course

Frontline is a church that makes a difference – to the lives of its members and to all that it serves. Here you will find all that Jesus offers – love, acceptance, forgiveness, friendship, help, hope and heaven.

The Rt Rev James Jones – Bishop of Liverpool

What you will read in Nic's manifesto are the values that have shaped Nic's character and have done so much to shape the character of Frontline Church. It is important that these values are constantly visited and embodied otherwise there is the danger of 'lapsing into style'. This phenomenon happens when people take on the style of a movement without taking on the values that have given rise to the movement.

Philip Vogel – Author and Leadership mentor, Pioneer Network

I have known Nic and Jenny Harding for over thirty years. No one has taught me more than they about how church can be relevant, exciting, passionate and full of impact. But more importantly, they showed me that buildings, leadership teams and programmes are incidental They showed me that the real deal is God's love – people expressing that love to one another and bringing a taste of heaven right into the here and now. Over two thousand years ago, Christians built community together, met in each other's houses, worshipped together, ate together and brought the good news of Jesus to their neighbours It was truly life changing. Nic has enormous experience of applying that model in today's world. This book distils that experience – I hope you enjoy it!

Chris Gillies – Chief Growth Officer, Zurich Insurance Company – Global Life

I was inspired, challenged, encouraged and motivated by Nic's book. I saw myself in a new light! I recognised that my work is probably my biggest contribution as a Kingdom servant. However, I learnt there's much more to do. After reading his book, you like me will be able to redefine your contribution to co-labouring in building the Church. I recommend it to you.

Chris Allen – Chief Executive of Forum Housing

As you read through this book you can clearly see the call of God on Nic's life and his passion to help shape the church to be all that God has called it to be. He speaks about these issues in depth and with insight coming from many years of church leadership. It has been my privilege to walk alongside him in this for the past twenty years.

Dave Connolly – Co-Senior Pastor of Frontline Church

Thanks

In writing this small book, I have trawled through the memories of many years' experiences. In the vast majority of those years I have been accompanied by my wonderful and very patient wife Jenny. None of this would have been possible without her support, encouragement and, at times, forgiveness. Thank you.

Along the way came four fantastic daughters, Chloe, Elli, Abi and Lizzie, who have put up with my many decisions that have shaped our journey, including leaving my career in general practice and the salary that went with it, and leaving Bristol – thank you. Thanks, too, to their husbands who have shared some of this journey with us in the church in Liverpool.

I am very grateful to a number of men and women of God who have mentored or encouraged me over the years: Ken Bufton, Dave Day, Steve Hepden, Phil Vogel, Dwight Smith, Jimmy Dowds and Chris Allen, to name but a few. Their insights and belief in me have made all the difference. Although I have never been mentored by Loren Cunningham, the founder of Youth With A Mission, I feel that, in many ways, my life has been shaped by his writing and example.

Thanks to those who gave input to the text at draft stages, especially John Gibson and John Cavanagh who had many helpful suggestions, most of which have been included. Nicky Gibson, Honor Allen, Anna Claridge and Grace Snow had the painstaking work of proofreading the text, which has been a great blessing.

Rhiannon Alexander, my long-suffering PA, has consistently been cheerful and amazingly helpful at every stage in updating the text, while keeping me well supplied with tea and coffee.

Ultimately, I thank Jesus for keeping me on this journey. It is only he who has sustained me in the darkest hours, and given me a vision of his church that is worth living and dying for. Thank you with all of my heart.

1. Beginnings

Sitting on the grass on an island in the middle of the River Seine in Paris, I was riveted by the speaker's tales. She spoke of hearing the voice of God, people having life-transforming encounters with Jesus, the amazing results of Spirit-led prayer and of people experiencing physical healing. I thought to myself, "It doesn't get any better than this."

This was the kind of vibrant New Testament Christianity I had been longing to experience for years. It was July 1973, and my life was about to change for ever.

Less than a week earlier I had been on the way back from my first year of university in Bristol with my gorgeous girlfriend (now my wife – how did I manage that?). We stopped off at Capel Bible week with some friends on our way back to Jenny's home in Folkestone to meet her parents.

My trusty little minivan had got us there safely and we settled down to hear the main speaker that night, someone I'd never heard of before. His name was Loren Cunningham. Thirteen years earlier he had started a mission organisation called Youth with a Mission[1], also known as YWAM – now the biggest mission organisation in the world.

I had never heard the likes of the stories that he told of God's miraculous response to acts of faith and generosity, and they struck a deep chord. After hearing his message on miracles through giving, Loren casually mentioned that there were places still available on a mission in Paris starting in a few days time. This was the kind of Christian life I had longed for ever since I had given my life to Christ as a 12-year-old in a field in West Runton, Norfolk.

God had spoken to me one evening in that field in an unmistakable way. Though not a dramatic audible voice, it was a clear call to know and follow the God we had been hearing about. As the light from the paraffin lamps cast a yellow hue over the straw-strewn ground, the speaker concluded his talk by asking us to close our eyes in prayer. And as he prayed, I heard another voice, a voice that was speaking to my heart.

That night I lay in my sleeping bag on the rough ground pondering what to do. Bob, my normally snoring tent buddy was also awake, and I tentatively broached my thoughts. To my relief, he had had a similar experience and we agreed together to find our "tent officer" the following morning to say that we wanted to become Christians. When we did so, he prayed with us to receive Christ. It was very simple and unpretentious, but from that moment on, I knew my future was bound up with God's plan for my life. No matter how hard I tried to ignore him during my teenage years, I could not escape this sense of calling.

Jesus held me through those turbulent teenage years. He kept me for himself, and put deep longings in my heart. I often wanted to rebel or deny him for personal convenience, but he held on to me.

My youth group leader was a great source of strength, as were other Christian friends at school. Arriving at university, everything began to fall into place with the opportunity to discover the dynamic Christian experience I was longing for.

After some quick planning, I arrived at my future father-in-law's house to leave my car and catch the flight from Ashford airport. I managed to block his lawnmower in the garage, which did not get me off to a good start in this important relationship! A few hours later I was on a Dan Air flight to Paris, such a primitive example of budget airlines that I was convinced that the door on the plane was held on with string and that it stayed aloft only by prayer.

The week was packed with teaching from the leaders in the morning and evening, and street evangelism in the afternoon, using my entire schoolboy store of O-Level French. It was both terrifying and exhilarating. There were so many stories of God touching people's lives through simple conversations. My own seemingly feeble attempts to share the good news of Jesus were used in ways that amazed me, and we felt we were discovering what we had been created for. Few of us were evangelistically gifted, but we all sensed the privilege and call of being ambassadors for Christ.

Having had such a life-giving experience in Paris, I signed up for the next YWAM mission I could go on. I ended up spending most of the rest of the summer holidays in Amsterdam on their houseboat called "the Ark." In the day we would go out on the streets, to Dam Square, and to the red light district, talking with any who would stop for us. In the evening the houseboat turned into a coffee bar and those we'd invited came and talked some more. It was my first real taste of living in community, with a role for everyone. My main contribution was cleaning the toilets, a job I took great pride in.

This was pivotal stuff. It was planting in my soul deep convictions about the priorities of the Christian life, including an unwavering commitment to be the bearers of the good news of Jesus to those who had not yet heard. That's probably why in 1991 when we came to plant a church in Liverpool, the only strap line I could think of (the name Frontline did not come until a couple of years later), was "Church with a Mission" – the grown-up version of Youth with a Mission.

Leaving Amsterdam behind, I arrived back in Bristol for my medical studies with new-found fervour. I was hungry for more of these destiny-inspiring experiences. Jenny and I sought out a church with real intimacy in worship. Most churches were still stuck in the "hymn sandwich" format. We were looking for Spirit-inspired teaching and somewhere the spiritual gifts were being used, but hardly any churches accepted that the gifts of the Spirit were for today, with the exception of the Pentecostal denominations. Most of those that did were started by people who had been kicked out of their previous churches for speaking in tongues – hard to imagine today.

I believe that the words church and mission should be inseparable

On the edge of the city we found a small group of people meeting together in the front room of a council house. This band of a dozen or so believers had come to faith mainly through the efforts of Hugh Thompson and Peter Lyne and their tent campaigns. Naturally speaking, two eager 19-year-old students had little in common with the worldly-wise residents of Patchway estate. And yet we immediately felt at home. We knew that we belonged there, and we didn't look back for the next 18 years.

This was my introduction to the house church movement[2], still in its infancy. Gifts of the Holy Spirit, creativity in worship, preaching that was revelation not just information, relationships and community, kingdom theology, women in leadership and many other ground-breaking truths and practices emerged in those early years. It was a heady time.

In the same year that Jen and I returned from our summer missions (she had been on a YWAM mission in London while I was in Paris), I received for the first time a revelation of what the church was meant to be. I was completely taken aback. Instead of viewing the church as an institution or a building, as irrelevant or just plain dull, I saw it as a victorious army, a healing family, a community of believers who had all things in common, a body where everyone had a crucial function, a temple made of "living stones" which God, by his Spirit would inhabit and fill, a beautiful bride that would be the envy of the world, a church that could complete the great commission and be prepared for Jesus' return. This revelation of the church was like dynamite, ready to explode!

As truth after truth unfolded in those coming months I knew what I was living for. I was spoiled for the ordinary. This church that Jesus died for and was coming back for, this church that was the hope of the world, this church that could be a foretaste of heaven, was quickly becoming my passion. What could I do in my lifetime to see such a church emerge? What could Jesus do with me and others like me who would commit their lives to such a cause? There seemed no limit to what God could do, and no reason not to pursue the dream.

So these twin revelations about mission and church became my spiritual DNA, informing my passions and shaping my life choices.

Imagine if groups of Christians all over the nation began to see church like this and lived it out in daily life

Shortly after coming back from Amsterdam, I approached my pastor to suggest I might want to give up my studies and go full time with YWAM. He wisely encouraged me to finish my medical course and reconsider at a later date what God might be saying about serving him. It was one of the best decisions I made, because studying and later becoming a GP was my pastoral and leadership training. I needed to grow up and learn about life. I am so grateful for those years of experience, which meant I actually had something to offer when God called me out of medicine at the age of 32.

I was hungry to learn and grow during those years. I was given my first leadership role as a 21-year-old, leading a small group. It was a steep learning curve. I soon joined the informal leadership of the church and was privileged to be mentored by Hugh Thompson and others. As I studied my Bible, read Christian books, talked to more mature Christians and went to conferences, I was getting the theological and biblical training I needed.

Most of my learning was "on the job," including planting three congregations and overseeing a separate church plant. I was learning while doing, surely the pattern that Jesus used with his disciples. Although studying theology full time at university or Bible school has many merits, it can have the disadvantage of cramming the brain full of information without the life context to test and shape it.

I believe that leaders are best trained on the job

Many other students followed Jen and me to the church in Bristol, and as we grew the centre of gravity geographically soon moved to nearer the centre of the city and the University. We had the magic ingredient of momentum. It felt as if we were unstoppable. Surely this wonderful church that I saw in my imagination was just around the corner.

Sadly, the great hope of the house church movement was never realised. In my opinion, we lost sight of the great commission mandate of reaching the lost. We naively believed that when the world saw the quality of love we had for each other they would come flooding in. They did not. With the exception of one or two house churches of that time (notably Ichthus Christian Fellowship) we all focussed more inwardly than outwardly. We failed to heed Archbishop William Temple's words, "The church is the only society that exists for the benefit of those who are not its members."

However, like all successful relay runners, the house church movement did pass on the baton of its rediscovered truths, including a vision for what the church could be, to a wider collection of churches both within and outside mainstream denominations. Those outside the traditional structures tended to be known as the "new churches," and many of the house churches morphed into these, or quietly faded away.

My own journey was later to take Jenny and me out of Bristol

I believe that any church will inevitably take on the DNA of its vision-casting leaders

and across my river Jordan – the Mersey – to the promised land of Liverpool. It would be a chance to start all over again with a magnificent band of ten other men and women who wanted to try and live out our conviction about mission, with our passion for church.

Our aim was to form a new body with this double helix of spiritual DNA.

Experience clearly shows that any church will grow around the conviction of its leaders and the vision they consistently cast. Those convictions will be affected by training, but mostly shaped by experience. Whatever the vision statement says, whatever the denominational affiliation, the church will take on the DNA of its leader or leaders. This is neither surprising nor bad; it's just how it happens. For us, the DNA was my conviction about mission and church.

Questions for discussion

- If you had to teach a new Christian about the church, what passage of Scripture would you use?
- What key truths would you highlight?
- What personal milestones would you use as examples to explain this reality?

Endnotes

1. www.ywam.org

2. The roots of the house church movement were in the charismatic renewal of the 1960s, but it began to gather momentum in the early 1970s. Some leaders had been politely told they were no longer welcome in their churches because they spoke in tongues; many of these were from the Plymouth Brethren. In many circles the use of the gifts of the Spirit was still hugely controversial and threatening. Those who left their churches began to meet in homes with other like-minded believers.

Other strands of the house church movement came from Pentecostals who were frustrated with the dead traditionalism of their churches and sought something fresh and real. Some just heard the call of the Spirit to try and model New Testament church all over again, as described in Acts 2:41-47.

The characteristics of the movement in the early days were strong relationships and community, the gifts of the Spirit, informality of style, lay leadership, everyone contributing to meetings, and new worship songs.

In time the house church movement gave way to the more broadly based "new church" movement of the 1980s and 90s, which included renewed denominational churches. The house churches tended to outgrow their original home-based meetings and started to meet in rented or purchased premises. They also started to form networks of churches headed up by "apostolic leaders."

Those that focussed outwards in reaching unchurched people generally did well. Others that remained inward looking did not thrive, and in some cases failed to survive.

2. So what is the church?

It was 1986. I pondered this question as I sat in my front room hunched over a cup of coffee, thinking about the congregation that I was involved in planting. Having moved to the area of Bishopston in Bristol, Jenny and I had pioneered a local congregation of our church. Over a couple of years it had grown to about eighty adults.

Five years earlier I had quite miraculously taken on a single-handed medical practice with over 3,000 patients. So now as a busy GP with four children all under the age of six, I was faced with some serious choices. I was effectively doing two full-time jobs, and my family was suffering, or to be more precise my poor wife was.

It seemed like God was giving me a choice – what did I want to do? What did I want to give my life to? The life of a GP was certainly attractive, I enjoyed the work, the kudos, the salary, the influence.

But something was calling me to serve the church, this amazing instrument devised by God to be the hope of the world. The same call I had felt as a 19-year-old was now coming back stronger and clearer at the age of 32.

So as the dregs of the coffee turned cold, I realised that I needed to understand what the church was, if I was to give the rest of my life to serving it.

In a simple moment of profound revelation, the thought came to me that the church was a "worshipping, witnessing community." We know that there is a reality called the church universal – that worldwide communion of all believers across all time that make up the church of Jesus Christ, but here I was beginning to see what the local expression of that church in time and place could look like.

I believe that the church is a worshipping, witnessing community

Certainly there can be a variety of expressions of church, from a small group meeting in a front room to a citywide gathering of believers, and many shapes and sizes in between. All of these would be served by this simple definition.

These three dimensions of church had become clear to me and have served me well as a working framework ever since. They relate closely to the triangle life-shape of "up, in and out" described by Mike Breen in his book *A Passionate Life*[1]. He describes the three key relationships in our lives as being "up" towards God ("worshipping"); "in" towards one another ("community") and "out" towards those outside the church ("witnessing").

The confirmation to my call to serve God in leadership in the church, and leave my medical career came soon after that light-bulb moment.

Ian Smale (also known as Ishmael) was leading an event in Bristol and we had offered him hospitality for the night. As we sat together over breakfast the next morning, he turned to me and said "You know, Nic, you're never going to catch men until you leave your nets." Ian knew nothing about my thoughts of leaving medicine and wanting to help lead the church. Neither was he aware that one of my main responsibilities would be in forming and leading a full-time evangelistic training team. His words created an explosion in my chest – an explosion of delight. God had spoken and confirmed my greatest desire. The time was now.

And so in due course I handed on my medical practice to two other fantastic GPs in the church who had become my partners. The medical practice continued to grow from strength to strength, and my new adventure began.

We all have a "call" on our lives to serve God in some specific ways. We may not be called out of regular secular work, but we will still all carry a sense of calling from the moment we are born again. We are born again for a purpose: "For we are God's handiwork, created in Christ Jesus to do good works, which God prepared in advance for us to do" (Ephesians 2:10).

Question for discussion:

What do you sense you are called to be and do?

Endnotes

1. Breen, M. and Kallestad, W., *A Passionate Life*, (NexGen, 2005)

3. The dimension that connects us with God

This first dimension, the upward dimension, connects us to God – the source of life, the one who directs and sustains his people. It is a dimension that is expressed in worship, prayer, biblical meditation, fasting and breaking bread, among many other activities. Worship is our highest calling as followers of Christ. This dimension causes us to walk in dependence on him, and do everything out of love for him.

The upward dimension is foundational to everything else. Without this, our lives will simply be like an unplugged electrical appliance or a car without petrol. The connection to God as a group of believers is vital. Without it we can only be two-dimensional, flat, lacking depth. We will be working in human strength, and running out of motivation when the going gets tough. At best we will be a happy club, at worst, a self-deluded cult.

Imagine if love was the motivation for all that we did for Christ

The upward dimension is our power source and place of correct perspective. Some say that if we have our head in the clouds we will be of no earthly use. But we need to be people with a heavenly perspective that enables us to see our circumstances from God's point of view. It's a place where fresh faith is received and a renewing and refreshing touch from God is experienced. It's also a vital place of mental and spiritual realignment.

We so quickly get caught in the trap of human thinking, secular standards, and cultural norms. We lose sight of the greatness of our God, the unlimited power at his disposal, and the incredible love and faithfulness that characterises his relationship with us. Worship allows us to regain that perspective. With our head above the spiritual clouds we can at least see that the Son is still shining on us.

I am passionate about worship, not only private and personal encounters with God as we offer him the praise and adoration that is due to him, but also the gathered worship of the saints. Those are times when as his bride-to-be we come in abandoned love and exuberant expressions of praise. Those are times when it seems that heaven has come among us and Jesus himself is walking among his people.

It troubles me when Christians have a casual, "take it or leave it" attitude to gathering together for worship. Although there is no prescribed way or time or frequency, the saints need to gather to host the presence of God, to worship the King of kings, and to be built up in the scriptures. I'm sure it must grieve God's heart when the reasons for our absence are self-centred or lazy – "Oh, we just fancied a lie-in," "There was a good football match on," "I had to have some me-time," "I wanted to go to the gym," or even the seemingly laudable, "We needed some family time." I'm not saying that any of these things are undesirable, but it's all too easy to slip into bad habits.

It has become part of our pick-and-mix culture. We listen to our favourite preachers on pod casts, our favourite Christian bands on iTunes or CDs, and maybe only attend a church gathering when there is some special event. But so often this simply reinforces our consumer mind-sets and our isolation from the body of Christ.

The joy of being together in one place and time, and for a brief moment having the opportunity to experience a little bit of heaven, is such a massive privilege. It is not surprising that the writer of Hebrews says, "And let us consider how we may spur one another on toward love and good deeds, not giving up meeting together, as some are in the habit of doing, but encouraging one another—and all the more as you see the Day approaching" (Hebrews 10:24-25).

When my attitudes have been casual, or when I have been preoccupied with the matters of the day, I have found it difficult to connect with the presence of God. When I have been proud or indulging my intellect, it has been a struggle to experience his love. But when I've come to the end of myself and become acutely aware of my need, then it has been like heaven rushing into my heart. It has been a delight to be in the Father's presence. It has been manna from heaven, food for my soul, and life to my body.

After the Ark of the Covenant, symbolising the very presence of God, had been stuck in the house of Obed-Edom for some years, King David decided to move it to Jerusalem. As he brought it into the city he danced before the Lord with complete abandonment, accompanied by the sound of shouting and trumpets (2 Samuel 6:12-16).

David also saw fit to establish a new form of worship in the tabernacle he set up at Jerusalem (1 Chronicles 16:1, 4-6). It involved singers and musicians ministering to the Lord twenty-four hours a day. David says in Psalm 22:3 that the Lord inhabits, or is enthroned on the praises of his people.

In Acts 15 at the council of Jerusalem, James, the leader of the church, quotes Amos saying that when the Lord returns he will rebuild the tabernacle of David (Amos 9:11). The original prophecy

Imagine if every time we gathered for worship, we were all conscious of his presence, Jesus walking among his people

from Amos was several hundred years before Christ came and the church was born.

Despite the fact that the Temple of Solomon was much more impressive, it was the tabernacle of David with its non-stop worship that was the image James used to describe God's heart and intention. Could this description be a clue to the kind of church, the dwelling of God in the Spirit (Ephesians 2:22) that we are invited to build and be part of today?

There is a hint in this passage in Acts that the Scripture also refers to a later return of the Lord, his second coming, when the worship of heaven will bear some of the hallmarks of David's tabernacle.

I believe that worship is the key to the presence of God

Many rightly point to the variety of expressions of worship beyond corporate singing. Yet I am persuaded that when the body of Christ gathers, singing is the most powerful way of expressing our worship and welcoming his presence among us. Singing harnesses the power of melody, harmony, speech, poetry, listening, emotion and whole body involvement. It is a powerful combination that is designed to open our hearts and minds to experience the reality of God's presence. The resurgence of choirs in recent times may reflect this longing and indicate the power of collective singing.

It is not by chance that in the book of Revelation we see heaven characterised by the singing of myriads of angels, the four living creatures, the twenty-four elders, every living thing, multitudes from every tribe, people and tongue, and those who had been victorious in spiritual battle (Revelation 5:8-14; 7:9-12; 15:2-4). It moves the heart of God as well as our own.

Although our main worship venue lacks good acoustics, I am regularly blown away by the power of our sung worship. There are times when it feels as if heaven has come down, or perhaps we have momentarily entered heaven!

While many instruments such as harps contributed to the worship of the tabernacle, it is clearly the singing that dominates the sound of heaven. I long for that great vocal sound, the sound of heavenly worship, to fill our gatherings. It's not surprising that we often see hearts melted and bodies healed, as well as minds renewed, in

I believe that abandoned, heart-felt, Jesus-centred, sung worship is the sound of heaven

the context of our corporate sung worship. Some call it mere music therapy, but there are lasting testimonies of changed lives after an encounter with God in worship.

During the worship at one of our conferences, a man who had suffered a stroke and still had residual weakness in one of his legs, felt the power of God touch his body and he was instantly healed.

In contrast to worship, praise has a dynamic of its own. It is often linked to spiritual warfare in Scripture. In Joshua 6 the Israelites are surrounding the city of Jericho. It is the sound of the trumpets and the shout of the people that brings down the wall of the city.

In 2 Chronicles 20 the armies of Moab and Ammon were besieging King Jehoshaphat in Judah. The Lord instructed him to put the singers at the forefront of the battle formation – imagine King's College choir in the front lines of the invasion of Iraq. As they began singing and praising, the enemy armies started to fight and destroy one another, until all were dead.

When Paul and Silas were in prison at midnight singing hymns of praise to God, a great earthquake shook open the prison doors. After persuading the jailer not to commit suicide, they baptised him and his household (Acts 16:25-32). The ability of praise to break down seemingly impregnable walls, to defeat the enemy's strategy, or to open prison doors, points to its great power.

In the summer of 1989 it seemed that the Lord allowed the enemy some leeway to test me to see if I really believed what I preached. It was a French Bible camp and I was speaking on praise and spiritual warfare. One night I had the most horrible nightmares involving body parts and blood-filled baths. I woke really disturbed and went to check on the children. They were all sleeping soundly, but I could not settle until I started to

I believe in the power of praise

pray and praise in tongues. Eventually peace returned and I was able to go back to sleep.

The following day I had just finished speaking when there was a great commotion further up the campsite. Eventually we were told to come quickly to reception, where we found our blood-soaked daughter. She had run through a plate glass door in the reception lobby that she'd failed to see, and had badly gashed her leg, with cuts on her stomach and just above one eye.

I cradled her in my arms as we dashed to the nearest hospital, praying and thanking God for his goodness and faithfulness while my daughter sobbed quietly. She was seen to quickly and repaired with 80 stitches, and miraculously there was no damage to major arteries, nerves, tendons or other organs. I thanked God for his deliverance and protection.

A day or two later during some free time we went with others to a nearby lake where I demonstrated my prowess at windsurfing. However, when it was time to leave I looked less clever when I realised my car keys were at the bottom of the lake. We could have panicked and ranted, looking for someone to blame, but instead we praised God for his presence and provision. As we did so, a Citroen mechanic appeared from nowhere and was able to fix the electrics so that at least we could shut the windows and lock the doors.

The problem was that the only set of spare keys was back in the UK, a bank holiday weekend was about to start and the chance of getting them before we were due to leave seemed slim. With minutes to spare, we got to the local post office before it closed and called neighbours in Bristol. Our friend was able to break into our house, retrieve the spare keys, and get them in the post just in time. The keys arrived the day before we were due to leave and all was well. The power of praise in response to the dream and the traumas that followed had been well and truly tested, and it had not been found wanting.

Prayer is obviously a vital part of this upward dimension. Prayer changes us and it also moves God's hand to act. In some mysterious way, when we pray according to God's will, he hears us, and when he hears us we know we have whatever we have asked of him (1 John 5:14-15).

Romans 8 says the Spirit helps us in our weakness when it comes to praying and interceding. The Spirit prays through us according to

Imagine if as God's people we responded to every difficulty with praise, and believed that God would break in

God's will and the one who hears the prayers knows the mind of the Spirit (Romans 8:26-27). So letting the Spirit pray through us is the most effective way of praying. This scripture says that the result is that God works all things together for good. In other words, things change for the better. Things take place that would not otherwise have happened. Situations that would have been disastrous are salvaged by the deliverance of God. History is created as we partner with God.

Ephesians 6:18 says we are to "pray in the Spirit on all occasions with all kinds of prayers and requests." I believe that this includes three types of prayer. The first is simply praying in our native language as the Holy Spirit leads us. Thoughts come into our mind as to what to pray for and how to pray.

Secondly, it includes praying in tongues. This is the Holy Spirit praying directly through us in the angelic language given to us by him. The Father knows what we are praying and answers our prayers. We probably won't know what we are praying, but we can ask God to give us an interpretation, and that allows us to pray in our own language as well as in tongues. I believe Paul refers to this when he says, "I will pray with my spirit but I will also pray with my mind" (1 Corinthians 14:15).

The third kind of praying in the Spirit is "groaning" or sometimes called "travail." It is directly referred to in the Romans 8 passage we started with. There is an excellent chapter in Dutch Sheet's book *Intercessory Prayer* on this[1].

Prayer is a team event as well as an individual activity. Many of the most powerful times of prayer that I have experienced have been in groups, when we have all been of the same mind and focussed on the same thing. In the early days of starting the church in Liverpool, we used to meet every week at seven in the morning. It was in those prayer times that the foundations of the church were laid. We have had other seasons of weekly 7am prayer meetings. I am always amazed just how the Spirit leads those times of prayer – an hour never seems enough!

How much prayer is enough? It's an impossible question to answer, but we know that every area of our lives and the life of the church needs to be saturated in prayer. Two mothers meeting for coffee and mutual encouragement, two workers in the same office, a project or department in the church, a missional community working out their plans, the senior leadership dreaming of what God wants to do in the next ten years: it must all be drenched, under-girded, infused with prayer. It is a vital part of the upward dimension.

I believe in the power of praise

Prayer of course blends perfectly with praise and worship. They were made to go together. The same verse that begins, "I will pray with my spirit, but I will also pray with my mind," continues, "I will sing with my spirit but I will also sing with my mind" (1 Corinthians 14:15). Our worship of God positions us perfectly to hear from heaven and be Spirit-energised to pray.

Breaking bread, or as it is sometimes called, communion or the Lord's Supper, is a mysterious part of our worship and fellowship with the Father. Scripture patterns this around a meal. It was first inaugurated in the upper room at the last supper when Jesus explained that he was about to die. He broke the bread with his twelve disciples and shared a cup of wine with them, telling them that they would also share in his body and blood, which was about to be broken and shed for them (Luke 22:17-20). He asked them to continue to do this in the future, as they remembered him.

Imagine if prayer simply became a way of life

The pattern was continued by the early church. Scripture says they devoted themselves to the breaking of bread and that they broke bread from house to house and took their meals together with great joy (Acts 2:42, 46). The tradition of more formalised communion services did not emerge until much later in the history of the early church when they were permitted to own buildings.

I believe that breaking bread is most meaningfully practiced in the context of a home as part of a meal

We break bread in our main worship services from time to time, but to me the most meaningful and even scriptural way to do it is in the context of a meal, and in a home where fellowship is part of the package.

I remember sitting in our flat when we were first married, enjoying the community that was growing in the church in those days. The thought crossed my mind that it would be wonderful if there was some symbolic way that we could express our commitment to each other and to our common identity. In a flash the revelation came, that that was exactly what we did when we broke bread together. So the act is not just a vertical one of remembering what Christ has done and being thankful; the sharing in the bread and wine also has a horizontal dimension, of sharing in a common identity and purpose.

Questions for discussion:

- Why is the upward dimension so important to the life of the church, and how does the enemy keep us from investing in it?

- How can we make praise and prayer a way of life, not just something we do with other Christians?

- What is your experience of breaking bread, and when has it been most meaningful for you?

Endnotes

1. Sheets, D., *Intercessory Prayer*, (Gospel Light, 1997)

4. The dimension that connects us with the world

In my depiction of church as "a worshipping, witnessing community," the second dimension is the outward dimension of witness. This was the tricky one for us back in the 1970s and 80s. I was convinced that it was key to the health and growth of the church community, but it was difficult to establish. The Greek word for witness in the New Testament is *martur*, from which we get the word martyr. Clearly, being a witness for Jesus is not just a walk in the park (though that might be a good place to engage with others!) and might actually involve some sacrifice or pain.

Peter and John were arrested for preaching the gospel in Jerusalem. When told to stop preaching, they simply said "we cannot stop speaking about what we have seen and heard" (Acts 4:20). What a great definition of what it means to be a witness! Clearly our connection to God and community life is intended to overflow and touch a needy world around us. In fact if we are truly experiencing the abundance of God's love, blessing, provision, and answered prayer, it should be impossible to stop us talking about it.

Sadly, many of us get so locked into our own needs or personal concerns that we fail to realise that health and life come as we reach out to others who don't yet know Christ. As Paul said to Philemon, "I pray that you may be active in sharing your faith so you will have a full understanding of every good thing we have in Christ" (Philemon 1:6).

If worship is our highest calling, then mission must be our most urgent assignment. God is well able to reach and save people, but he has chosen us to be his hands and feet connecting with others on his behalf. He is full of compassion for a world that is alienated from him. He loved the world so much that he became a man, allowing himself to be tortured and put to death so that we could be reconciled to him. It was so that others could enjoy abundant life with him here, and for eternity in heaven. We are the missing link, and in some cases, the weakest link!

The church in the UK has fortunately, to a large extent, rediscovered its mission mandate in the last fifteen years. The cynic might say that it has had to do so in the face of potential extinction. Phrases like "mission-shaped church," "missional community," and "missionary congregation" have become much more normal than they were twenty years ago.

There has always been a faithful remnant of churches waving the flag of mission. Some of these have been run by leaders with evangelistic gifting, but now many more are led by those with teaching, pastoral, prophetic or apostolic gifts. They are becoming strongly outwardly focussed as a result of biblical and eschatological (end-times) convictions, not just personal preference or style. I am greatly encouraged by this trend.

Back in the 1970s and 80s with the rediscovery of community and kingdom in the house-church movement which we were a part of, the emphasis was on building the church,

I believe the church exists for its non-members

and discovering a new ecclesiology (way of doing and being church). As vital though this was, it distracted us from reaching the lost. I seemed to be unable to do anything about it and the more I talked about reaching out, the more I seemed to alienate people, probably due to my own self-righteousness. It was partly this longing to see the church reaching out that caused me to give up my medical career and work full time as part of the church leadership team in Bristol.

As well as planting new congregations, we also set up a full time training team in evangelism – the Frontline Team. I hoped that this would provide a much-needed stimulus to the church. The team began with about six young people taking a gap year to be trained and involved in evangelism in Bristol, other UK cities, and overseas. The final team five years later was about twenty strong. We had a great time.

A young man wandering through the city centre heard us singing and preaching and stopped to listen. He was a chef on leave from his ship in the merchant navy. His life had no meaning and he was feeling suicidal. He came to church with us and gave his life to the Lord, losing all that sadness. He later joined us on mission trips to Greece where his own experience was a powerful testimony to the many sailors who we met off the ships in Piraeus.

Another passer-by in Bristol, a young woman in her early twenties, stopped to listen to our feeble attempts to draw a crowd. She leant on a nearby tree and just seemed to be taking it all in. When one of the team went over to talk to her we quickly discovered that her intentions were anything but innocent. She proudly declared that she was a witch from a coven in Pucklechurch and was now controlling us with her mind. I did not doubt that she was genuinely into witchcraft, but questioned her ability to manipulate what we were doing.

After a while Jim, who was talking to her, started to get quite animated so I thought that as the team leader I ought to go and check out what was going on. As I started to talk to the girl, Jim started to pray in tongues. She immediately turned on him saying quite venomously, "What's that? What are you saying?" Jim carried on regardless and she became more and more worked up, till eventually her whole body was contorted with anguish and her fists clenched.

Finally she collapsed in a heap on the ground, and I was quite glad there were no passing policemen at that point. She had obviously experienced a powerful deliverance and we had the privilege of taking her into the nearby John Wesley chapel and leading her to Christ.

It was in such situations that we discovered a deep sense of fulfilment in reaching out with the good news about Jesus. It was as though we were connecting with what we had been created for. None of us were natural evangelists, but in obedience to the great commission we were finding great joy and a sense of approval from the Father. It was deeply fulfilling and at times completely exhilarating.

With these and plenty of similar stories, I had hoped that the church would catch the excitement of being outwardly focussed. But somehow

Imagine if every member of the church carried the DNA for mission

instead of the whole church getting a vision for reaching out to their friends and neighbours, it was almost as though people concluded, "Well, the Frontline team are doing it, so there's no need for me to be worrying about it." I learnt an important lesson that day: if it's not in the DNA of the church, it's very hard to make it happen.

The whole message of the kingdom, powerfully proclaimed and demonstrated by Jesus, is one of taking ground, reclaiming broken lives and waste places. The kingdom advances primarily by winning the hearts and minds of those separated from God. It moves forward one soul at a time.

As people turn to the Lord, the kingdom starts to affect whole families, communities, schools, workplaces, even cities. Jesus said, "From the days of John the Baptist until the present time, the kingdom of heaven has endured violent assault, and violent men seize it by force [as a precious prize – a share in the heavenly kingdom is sought with most ardent zeal and intense exertion]" (Matthew 11:12, Amplified Bible).

The gospel is one of words, works and wonders. It must be proclaimed both in love and in truth, and must be demonstrated both in acts of kindness and acts of power. Our outreach can be individual and collective. Many of our Frontline projects have been bridges for others to cross over to an experience of Jesus and involvement in his church.

I believe that the gospel should be experienced in words, works, and wonders

A number who have experienced God's touch through our Healing Rooms ministry have come to faith and joined the church. Many children in our Kidz Klub programme have accepted Christ and subsequently become part of the youth and then the young adults in church. Whether it is the Sticky Fingers parent and toddler group; Streetwise, befriending the sex workers; Inform, the pregnancy crisis service; or CAP, our debt advice service, all are powerful demonstrations of the love of God. And when questions are asked, then the truth can be shared.

Jesus was clear on his mission. After forty days of intense battle with the enemy, he stood up in the synagogue, and read from the prophet Isaiah, "The Spirit of the Lord is on me, because he has anointed me to preach good news to the poor. He has sent me to proclaim that freedom for the prisoners and recovery of sight for the blind, to release the oppressed, to proclaim the year of the Lord's favour" (Luke 4:18-19, Isaiah 61:1-2).

The disciples were so amazed at his preaching and miracles that they tried to persuade him to stay at Capernaum, where he had just healed Simon Peter's mother-in-law. You can imagine the disciples trying to make Jesus the first pastor of Capernaum Community Church. Jesus' reply says it all, "I must preach the Kingdom of God to the other cities also, for I was sent for this purpose" (Luke 4:42-44). As with the apostle Paul, the gospel compelled him to go.

When Jesus is speaking to Zacchaeus, he says "The Son of Man came to seek and save what was lost" (Luke 19:10). On another occasion, after Jesus' resurrection he says to his disciples, "As the Father has sent me, I am sending you" (John 20:21). His last words to his disciples in the other gospels reinforce the urgency of the task (Matthew 28:18-19, Mark 16:15-18, and Acts 1:8. Acts is the continuation of Luke's gospel). For us to disregard this priority would be to deny the power of Jesus' words, and to withhold the bread of life from a hungry world.

Just before Jenny and I left Bristol, I went to say goodbye to some friends called Adrian and Judy. I realised that in all our fun times

I believe in a church whose primary assignment is to reach the least, the last, and the lost

together over several years, I had never really taken the opportunity to share the gospel with them. I was embarrassed to spring on them matters of eternal significance just before leaving and eventually just waded in, saying, "This may seem a bit weird but ..." To my great surprise, they responded, "Nic, if this is so important, why haven't you told us before?" I was devastated to think I had nearly missed sharing the good news with two open hearts, just to avoid awkwardness. I determined never to make that mistake again.

And so we came to Liverpool, with a clear mission "to seek and save that which was lost," to be the good news wherever we were. Hence our strap line: "Church with a Mission." The church has retained that priority and it has remained a clear distinctive in all our years of change and growth. Our vision statement says, "We see multitudes of men, women and children turning to Christ and becoming true disciples."

Questions for discussion:

- Why is the outward dimension usually the weakest in any church or community?

- Explain the relationship between words and actions when it comes to reaching out with the good news.

- What is the message of the kingdom?

Endnotes

1. Kidz Klub is a ministry at Frontline Church modelled on Bill Wilson's Metro Ministry in Brooklyn, New York. It has been running for 17 years and trained many other teams in the UK to set up similar ministries. Over the years many thousands of kids have been through the club, and hundreds of thousands of home visits have been made.

5. The dimension that connects us with each other

This third dimension is the inward dimension that results in genuine community being established. That community aspect was finding many expressions in the house church movement of the 1970s and early 80s. Graham Pulkingham wrote the book *They Left their Nets*[1] chronicling the amazing miracles of individual transformation, as the Church of the Redeemer in Houston, Texas, experimented with community living. It was something that we also aspired to, as we read of the early church in the book of Acts.

We were in and out of each other's houses, enjoying a level of honesty and care that was uncommon in churches at that time, and sharing belongings with each other. We wanted every person who joined the church to experience that type of community and find belonging, healing and identity within it.

If you have ever tried it, it's not that easy. Over-familiarity, petty annoyances, comparison, and offence, differences in standards, child-care values and lifestyle choices were all the seeds of discontent in an otherwise perfect community. The ethos that "They did not count anything they owned as belonging to them" (Acts 4:32) was fine if you were always on the receiving end, but harder if you were the one sharing your possessions, your car or opening up your home to others. Lending out my tools has always been a challenge for me.

Somehow we muddled through and continued to find ways of making it work. Maybe we could never have the communal experience of the Acts 4 church, without Acts 4 persecution. But community was definitely on the agenda for our model of church, and there was a measure of equality without the uniformity of communism.

Belonging is of course a very human need – one created by God. The heart of every person longs for meaningful connection with others, to love and be loved. We long to be truly known by others and then accepted for who and what we are. Loneliness is one of the great sadnesses of our time.

The statue of Eleanor Rigby sits outside one of our shopping centres in Liverpool. She sits alone, a reminder of "all the lonely people" living lives of quiet desperation. In a world of over six billion people, how can that be? How is it, in a society that is more electronically connected than we ever thought possible, that individuals seem less able to make real meaningful relationships? The void is so often filled with alcohol, drugs, career, busyness, the internet, and hedonism. Sexual pursuit and intensity of experience has become a substitute for true intimacy in human relationships.

When God said that it was not good for man to be alone (Genesis 2:18), he was not just thinking about marriage, but the wider community that would grow out of family. Family will always be the basic building block of community, but we still have a lot to learn about family. We tend to think of our culture as normal[2]. But our culture is not normal.

Biblical Jewish culture was very much the model of extended family and is probably nearer God's heart for family and community. Certainly extended families are much more common globally than our typical western unit of nuclear or single parent family.

For the last 35 of our 36 years of marriage, Jenny and I have always had people live with us, some just for convenience, some to help us with childcare in the early years, some to find healing or safety, others because they had nowhere else to go. But for all those years Jenny and I have found it an enriching and rewarding experience. It has certainly reduced the number of rows we would otherwise have had! At one point, there were 18 of us under one roof. Life has never been boring in our house.

One particular young woman, Dianne, lived with us for several years. She had not had the best of experiences growing up, and came as a very broken girl with many needs. She loved our children dearly and was a great help to Jenny in those physically exhausting early childhood years, in the dark ages, when all nappies were washed by hand. With our four children under six years old, she made a huge difference, giving as much as she received.

What Dianne took away with her was the knowledge that she was loved for who she was, the confidence that she could make something of her life (which she now has done), and a family that would always have an open door for her. Recently, she made contact again while going through a difficult time; our relationship had stood the test of twenty years.

While doing a six-month junior hospital job in psychiatry, I met Martha, a young girl who was severely anorexic. Without thinking about it we asked her to come and live with us – it must have been strictly against doctor-patient protocol! Martha only lived with us for

I believe in the healing power of family and community

a few months and we already had three others in a small terraced house, along with our first two children, but it was the beginning of a healing process that continued as she lived with others in the church. She went on to marry a great Christian man and to have several children, which naturally speaking would have been unlikely given how she had abused her body.

So many today are growing up in one-parent households or blended families where there are real challenges to establishing identity and security. Could extended households, or at least meaningful involvement in "biblical community," be places of healing for many broken individuals?

Christian faith was never meant to be a solo sport, but a team game. The individualisation of faith has tended to mirror society's isolation and idolisation of the individual. Our changing values – the "What's in it for me?" attitude – have further shattered our communities. Serving the god of personal choice and the "rights culture," we object to taking responsibility for ourselves, let alone others and the inconvenience that it brings. "Me and my family" is the new Christian idol, to be protected against all intruders.

Hear my heart. I am not against strong family units – they are vital – but they are also all the richer for being inclusive and welcoming to others. What is our response to the question, "Am I my brother's keeper?" Will we embrace the implication of Psalm 68:6, "God sets

Imagine if every home practiced hospitality or was able to include those struggling with life

the lonely in families"? Mature community cannot be fully developed without families at the heart of it.

We believe that the values of community must be at the heart of the church. They are the heartbeat of the body, the expression of the interconnectedness that the body requires to function and express the life of Christ to the world. Jesus prayed that we would be one, even as he and the Father were one, so that the world might believe (John 17:21).

In Frontline we are seeking to build mid-sized missional communities. These are groups of people who have come together around a specific mission focus, interest, or area of commonality. Each one is intended to model all of the dimensions of Up, In and Out[3]. We see them as the primary place of belonging and outreach, which will complement the larger Sunday gatherings. Not-yet-believers will find a place of acceptance and welcome before they have ever crossed the line into the Kingdom of God. It is said, "People need to belong before they believe, and certainly before they behave like Christians." Let's ensure that our churches are places of inclusion, valuing the individual, and giving hope to broken people.

I was thrilled to visit one of the communities that has an arts theme and calls itself Studio. I went to their monthly creative writing evening and produced the first poem I had written for thirty years! What excited me was the great mix of believers and non-believers, the very real friendships and the fun that was had by all. In this kind of environment those who are seeking have a very natural opportunity to meet Christians and begin their journey of discovery.

I am also conscious that there are many who, for whatever reason, choose to keep themselves separate from the church body. Maybe they attend occasionally, but never commit. Others hop from church to church, avoiding the difficult conversations that come when you try to work out life together. Others get offended and walk away from church altogether.

It is the strategy of the enemy to isolate individuals and pick them off, like a lion isolates the weak and young from the herd before attacking them. Jenny and I have seen a number of couples walk away from church only to discover that their relationship comes under strain as the protection and support that the community affords is removed. Many have gone on to divorce and some then tragically lose their faith as well.

A generation of young people are emerging who find relationships difficult, who are not always in touch with reality, and who are reluctant to take responsibility for their lives or for others. Many of this Facebook generation have retreated from the pain of fractured families into a

I believe in the need for spiritual parenting

cyber reality where they can hide behind a persona of their own creation. They often fail in real relationships and retreat into a make-believe world. Instead of discovering the joy of belonging they make do with on-line relationships and phoney identities.

It is likely to become more difficult to build genuine community in the coming decades as more and more people reach adulthood without having had healthy relationships modelled to them at home. Only the church can fully address these issues because only God can heal these wounds. The battle to belong is real and for many it is painful. The need for spiritual mothers and fathers has never been greater.

Questions for discussion:

- Why does God want us to be part of an authentic community?

- Why do people get isolated from church and end up on the outside?

- How does the inward dimension address some of the brokenness of our society?

Endnotes

1. Pulkingham, G., *They Left their Nets: A Vision for Community Ministry*, (Hodder and Stoughton Limited, 1974)

2. We see our culture as "normal" much as we like to think of ourselves as the definition of "balanced" – we see ourselves as the centre point of all opposing extremes, and therefore see others as needing to come nearer to our centre of gravity to find equilibrium in their lives.

3. Breen, M. and Kallestad, W., *A Passionate Life,* (NexGen, 2005)

MANIFESTO

6. The power of contribution

One of the joys of leading a church is seeing people who lack confidence, have no idea about their gifts, and think that they can never make a difference, discover their unique and significant contribution.

Who wants to merely warm a pew on a Sunday or be just a name on a membership roll? Who wants to feel an insignificant lost soul in the crowd? No one. We all want to feel like our life counts for something, that we are making a

I believe in the power of everyone's contribution

difference and that we are playing to our strengths. And this is the life that God intended for us. We all have genuine God-given needs for security, self-worth and significance.

He created us with a unique design and for a specific purpose. Ephesians 2 verse 10 says "For we are God's workmanship, created in Christ Jesus for good works, which God prepared in advance for us to do." This reminds me of the Blue Peter catchphrase, "Here's one I made earlier." Each one of us has a calling on our lives, a destiny of "good works" waiting to be taken hold of. May our hearts echo Paul's words to the Philippians, "I press on to take hold of that for which Christ Jesus took hold of me" (Philippians 3:12). Your life has purpose and meaning when you discover your unique contribution.

Wouldn't it be great if every church made it a priority to develop the individual talents of every member? We are all so outstandingly different, and no two contributions are the same.

From the earliest days of my house church experience, there was always an expectation that each person would contribute something. Initially this would have been around the idea of everyone contributing to a meeting, as described in Colossians 3:16, "Let the word of Christ dwell in you richly, as you teach and admonish one another with all wisdom, and as you sing psalms, hymns and spiritual songs." And 1 Corinthians 14:26, "When you come together, each of you has a hymn, a word of instruction, a revelation, a tongue or an interpretation. Everything must be done so that the church is built up."

The use of spiritual gifts was revolutionary in those exciting pioneering days. Hearing God speak and seeing God minister through us was heady stuff, and definitely something we want to rediscover today.

When we began to develop our vision for the new church in Liverpool, one of our early statements of purpose was "We want Frontline to be a vision-led, outwardly-focused, every-member ministry church." We have sought to maintain that distinctive ethos over the years.

After two years of no church growth, in 2009 we took the radical decision to close all our cell groups and develop a new model of doing church: missional communities. We were looking seriously at what God might be saying about our lack of growth and sought to address all the factors, but one of the most significant was our cell structure. The model had served us well for five years – we had grown from 350 to 1000 people between 2002-2008 – but it was now beginning to stifle us. Though the cells were wonderful and life-giving for many, for an increasing percentage they restricted the development of leadership and gifts.

Many felt pressed into a shape that was not their natural fit, and others believed that they were called to lead but could not see how their gifts fitted the structure of cell leadership. This was a blow to us as we had firmly believed that cell groups were a model capable of indefinite multiplication, as they have been in the Latin culture of Colombia. It was hard to admit the need for change, but it would have been a mistake to continue with something that no longer served our needs.

Missional communities have given us a whole new approach to individual contribution and leadership development. Whereas before it was all dependent on one leader, now there can be a leadership team, with so many ways to make a unique contribution. Each missional community can be like a "church in the house" as described in Philemon 1:2, Colossians 4:15, Romans 16:5, a place where everybody gets involved.

The main Sunday celebrations have a more limited opportunity for this type of contribution. You may have heard of the phrase "fridge rights" for family members who visit home and help themselves to whatever they fancy in the fridge. In our Sunday gatherings some automatically have what I call "microphone rights," because of their role or seniority. But there must always be room for the unexpected contribution and for God to speak or move through anyone that he chooses. May we be sensitive to those times!

There are all sorts of volunteering opportunities that arise in the life of the church – it does take over one hundred people's input to make our services run over a period of a month, from set up, technical support, welcoming and playing in a worship band on a Sunday, helping with the children's groups, befriending, administrative support or video production. When people have less demanding jobs or are free of the pressures of small children, there are brilliant opportunities for developing gifts and talents. The chance to enhance a CV and learn new skills can be a great blessing to individuals as they serve the church.

However while some will undoubtedly contribute to the life of the church, their main sense of calling will be to the work place or in public life. It will be part of a society-transforming agenda, seeing areas like business, government, media, arts and entertainment, education, religion and the family infiltrated and changed from the inside. Added to these seven arenas would be many others like health care, law and order, sports and leisure.

In 1975 Loren Cunningham, the founder of YWAM, and Bill Bright, the founder of Campus Crusade, met for lunch in Colorado. They found that God had given them near identical words for the future as they shared with each other. They realised that if any nation was to be fully reached and transformed, then seven spheres or "mountains" would need to be infiltrated or conquered[1]. A month later Francis Schaeffer, the founder of the L'Abri Fellowship and great Christian philosopher of the twentieth century, said something almost identical.

Thus began a whole new emphasis known broadly during the 1980s and 90s as Kingdom theology. In fact, this theology had been pioneered by Calvin in Geneva in the 1500s. He recognised that the kingdom is bigger than the church, and has its impact wherever citizens of that kingdom are sent and planted. The sons of the kingdom that Jesus spoke of in Matthew 13:38 were intended not to just turn up at church and play a role there, but to be sent out into the world as agents of transformation.

Imagine if everyone knew how to make their best contribution and were committed to do so

Those who are called to be the yeast that leavens the whole batch of dough (Matthew 13:33) need to be connected, supported and identified with the local church; they need it for their own sake and for the sake of the church. It's too easy to become so "out there" that the rocket launched with great fanfare finds itself unable to return to planet earth and in the end gets lost in space, with only the tag "Christian" to show for itself.

We must find a way to both release and support those who have such callings. They are vital to the advance of the Kingdom and to preparing the church for Jesus' return. They are pioneers, perhaps even apostolic, but in a different context than church. As pastors we need special understanding of their role.

I remember many years ago having a friend come to me asking whether he should pursue a career in the life assurance industry or in church leadership. He was clearly so gifted that he could have done either. In that moment I had a bit of a revelation and said, "You would be wasted in church leadership," despite not wanting to downplay the importance and difficulty of church leadership. Over the next 25 years he rose to the top of his profession and is now very influential internationally in that field.

I believe that gifts are given not just for the church, but for use in the world

A couple of members of Frontline have been elected to be city councillors. This is not only a great privilege, but is also a great opportunity to serve God's kingdom agenda. Such folk need the support and encouragement of others in the church. We need to understand that if they have to attend important council committee meetings, then they can't be at every small group meeting.

I believe that we should all contribute to the life of the church, but that some have a greater capacity for that than others. Imagine if the Prime Minister was in your church – you'd have different expectations than you would of a student or nine-to-five worker. You might not expect the PM to go on the preaching rota. His or her primary contribution would be in another arena, like running the country.

One of our favourite questions is "How can you make your best contribution?" There is a danger that our gifts, ministry and role are seen to be all about "me" but Paul says that we use our gifts for the good of the body (1 Corinthians 12:7). The well-known challenge by President John F Kennedy, "Ask not what your country can do for you, ask what you can do for your country," applies to the church too.

There are many ways to discover our gifts, our best contribution. We have found that just asking some simple questions can reveal a lot. What do you enjoy doing? What have you been good at in the past? What have others said you are good at? Look for patterns in the answers to these questions.

If you enjoy opening your home and providing food for people, maybe you have a gift of hospitality. If you love being with people and helping them, maybe you have a gift of encouragement. If you see the roots of people's issues before they have admitted they have a problem, may be you have a counselling gift. If you love fixing and mending things, maybe you have a gift of...fixing things. It's not rocket science, is it?

The power of contribution is not only what it does for the church or organisation, but what it does for the individual. It is the fastest way to promote spiritual growth. The stimulus of knowing that others are relying on you is enough to put the fear of God into anyone, and cause them to press into God for their own personal development.

We are fulfilled in seeing our gifts developed in our own God-given way. I sometimes think I must be the luckiest man alive to spend my time doing what I am passionate about, and getting paid for it. A bored Christian should be an oxymoron, a contradiction in terms. There is no unemployment in the Kingdom of God. Most of us will be volunteers; a few will be paid for our contribution. Either way there is every opportunity to serve and be used by God to make a difference in the context of the church and its mission.

There are plenty of other more structured approaches to discovering your best contribution. The many variations of spiritual gift questionnaires can help, but it is within the rather narrow limits of specific gifts that are mentioned in the Bible. Peter Wagner has written extensively about this.[2]

The book *Now Discover your Strengths,*[3] by Marcus Buckingham and Donald Clifton, and the online Strengthsfinder questionnaire[4] that comes with it, is much broader in scope. It includes a section on how to manage and get the best out of people with particular strengths. It is a profound relief to many to discover that the way they are wired is a strength when applied in the right way. It is a revelation to others to suddenly understand that their colleague's behaviour is a reflection of a God-given quality, not just an irritating habit!

Delving deeper with Myers-Briggs personality type assessments,[5] or the Keirsey version,[6] can also add greatly to our self-understanding and help pave the way for greater self-awareness in our relationships or work environment. Some of the assessment tools are free online. The Belbin[7] team role preferences tool is another useful way of helping teams learn to play to each other's strengths.

When God made man and woman we have the profound statement, "in the image of God he created him, male and female he created them" (Genesis 1:27). Even before sin spoiled God's creation, it was impossible for one human to fully represent God. It was going to take at least one man and one woman.

In fact it takes a whole body of members to make Christ visible on earth. We are the body of Christ; he remains the head and we are his body. We together can represent, literally re-present him to the world. What a joy it is to find the body parts that we are to work next to, and discover that it's OK not to be any good at something because someone else is.

One of my personal joys is to work with my co-pastor Dave Connolly. We could not be more different, which does lead to tensions sometimes. Dave loves crisis, I love process. Dave is energised by being with people; I am energised by ideas, vision and strategy. Dave is not afraid of confrontation; I am better in counselling. Dave is looking for impact; I am looking for influence. Together we make up one good leader! Jesus sent his disciples out in twos, and had a good reason for doing so. The mix of the apostolic and the prophetic is vital for planting a church which has the potential to create a movement, not just a local institution[8].

In the Christian life, it's as a team that we will win. The only hero and celebrity is Jesus; there is no place for Christian superstars. Humility was the hallmark of Jesus on earth and should be of his followers today. The cult of celebrity must not influence the church today. We must make room for each other, defer to each other and learn from each other. We need each other.

In a game of football, when one man's ego dominates the play, the rest of the team does not get a look in. If the team wins there is little joy, and if it loses, there is no commiseration. That's not how the game is meant to be played. Even though I am not an expert, I can tell when a team is passing the ball around well, creating opportunities for each other and scoring as a result of great teamwork. Then the team spirit is a force to be reckoned with and the celebrations are shared by all.

The outcome of our joint contribution is immensely powerful. When the church plays to its strengths and each of us plays our part we are unstoppable. When we can draw on the amazing gifts of each other, we have unlimited potential to influence, to make an impact and to

I believe that together we can change the world

advance. Our mission in Frontline is "to build a vibrant church of whole-hearted Christ-followers, committed to unlimited growth and influence."[9] This is only possible if we all commit to making our best contribution.

The Pareto principle is the 80/20 rule. Twenty percent of the sales force gets 80% of the business; 20% of the effort gets 80% of the results; 80% of the problems come from 20% of the people, and so on. In church it is widely thought that 20% of the members make 80% of the contributions. This must not be so. We must be committed to helping every individual to discover and fulfil their potential, to pull their weight and to find their place on the team.

If we are not sure of our individual gifts, we can still offer our time and energy. Serving is actually a great way of discovering what we are good at. So don't wait until you are confident of every nuance of your gifting, just muck in. There's joy in simply being a part of a team and getting on with whatever needs doing. Faithfulness is much underrated. Jesus said "It is more blessed to give than to receive" (Acts 20:35).

In a larger church like Frontline, there must of course be many smaller teams, hence our mid-sized missional communities. Each one has the opportunity to build their own leadership team and discover how each person can use their gifts for the benefit of the community. Each community is like a family with purpose, and every gift is needed. The desire to grow is inherent in families: every good family raises its children to succeed in life and to make their mark; so too in our communities.

Through a network of small groups within each community we can love and support each other, spurring on one other to grow and use our gifts. Through relationships of accountability, we are regularly challenged as to how we are contributing.

The community enables us to use our gifts in all three dimensions – up toward God in worship, prayer and devotion, in toward each other in care, personal development, community building, teaching and organisation, and out in evangelism, creativity, hospitality, and of course in so many other ways.

Some gifts require a larger stage and therefore will also function beyond the communities. Some people will give their working time as paid or volunteer staff. Wherever gifts are used, there will be an energising and joy that comes with it. If this is never the case, then it's a sure sign that we are not operating in our God-given gifts or strengths, and it's time to ask some serious questions.

So enjoy discovering and making your best contribution. You will have the joy of growing in your gifts, being a part of team, and knowing that you are making a difference.

Questions for discussion:

- Why does the church depend on every person making their best contribution?

- In what way does everyone contribute to the life of the church?

- How are home-based meetings important for people's contribution?

Endnotes

1. www.reclaim7mountains.com

2. Wagner, P.C., *Discover your Spiritual Gifts*, (Regal Books, 2005)

3. Buckingham, M. and Clifton, D., *Now Discover your Strengths*, (Pocket Books, 2004)

4. www.strengthsfinder.com

5. www.myersbriggs.org

6. www.keirsey.com

7. www.belbin.com

8. For more thoughts on this, see chapter 10

9. "Our mission is to build a vibrant church of wholehearted Christ-followers committed to unlimited growth and influence. We are committed to reaching individuals, building church, transforming our city and impacting nations." To view our full vision statements, go to the Frontline website: www.frontline.org.uk

7. The discipleship journey

I confess I am an activist! To me, too much contemplation, personal reflection, self-appraisal and heart searching can all get a bit dull, unless I see it as part of my journey of adventure. We need to see that the learning process is intrinsically linked to our activities. We must learn to value the peace and joy that comes from becoming more Christ-like. We must come to that point in life where we realise that it's not about what I can do for God, but what God can do in and through me.

After a few decades (some of us are slow learners) I have come to realise that he is more committed to changing me than using me. I have wanted to serve God ever since I gave my heart to him in that field in Norfolk in 1966. I have always savoured the thought of the "Well done, good and faithful servant . . . Come and share your master's happiness," that will come to those who use their talents well in his service (Matthew 25:23).

The French theologian John Calvin (1509-1564) emphasised the sovereignty of God in choosing who would be saved, whereas the Dutch theologian Jacobus Arminius (1560-1609) emphasised our responsibility and free will to choose to follow Christ. The tension between the Arminian and the Calvinist position is expressed in the simple image of the gateway to Heaven. The words engraved over the stone archway as we walk through say, "Everyone who calls on the name of the Lord will be saved" (Acts 2:21), but on the other side, looking back from heaven, we see the inscription, "You did not choose me, but I chose you" (John 15:16).

As a card-carrying Arminian, I find it easier to look at the plight of the lost and want to finish the job of world evangelisation and see Jesus come back. It's harder for me to rest in his unchanging plan, feel comfortable in my salvation or accept that apart from him I can do nothing. Yet perhaps from heaven's perspective I will acquiesce to the Calvinist view after all. While I do passionately believe in the urgency of the task and our call to sacrificial service, I am increasingly convinced of the shortness of this life compared with eternity. Ultimately God is preparing us for our eternal relationship with him.

This earthly life is our preparation for life in our resurrection bodies. It seems that the degree to which we have conformed to his character-forming process will determine the quality and perhaps proximity of relationship we will enjoy with him in eternity (Luke 14:7-9, 2 Corinthians 5:9-10). Nevertheless I can't believe that any of us will be disappointed with heaven!

If I have the potential to affect either my reward, based on my contribution, or my relationship with him, then I want to take full advantage of the opportunity here and now. He is transforming us into his image (2 Corinthians 3:18). Being conformed to his image (Romans 8:29) means to be re-shaped to his form, his pattern, his beauty, his maturity, and his character.

Jesus says in Luke 13:24 to "Make every effort to enter through the narrow door, because many, I tell you, will try to enter and will not be able to." There is hard work and intense focus involved in becoming a disciple. We cannot be Jesus' disciple if we do not carry our own cross and come after him (Luke 14:27). None of this takes away from God's grace in saving and sanctifying us, because without it we are helpless and hopeless. But it clearly requires our co-operation to see it through, and not be like one of those spoken about in Hebrews 6:4-6, who fall away.

What would be the point of this process if it did not also have some eternal benefit? We know that to have a Christ-like character has many tangible benefits in this life. Enjoying peace of mind, freedom from anxiety, successful relationships, plus the joy of being close to Jesus are great rewards. But it's encouraging to think that the transformation we undergo in this life may contribute to our enjoyment of heaven.

With over 44 years of "being conformed" to his image and with so much further to go, I realise that the process rarely happens when all is well and we are seeing success in what we are doing. It usually happens when the pressure is on, when we have experienced failure, when **I believe that life is preparation for eternity** we are criticised unfairly, when we face opposition or persecution, when circumstances seem to be conspiring against us, sometimes when God seems a million miles away.

Some call it the school of hard knocks. When Jenny and I were in Bristol we worked in the local prison for a while. Inmates who became Christians naturally looked to us for help when they came out, and some of us who lived close by offered accommodation. One particular ex-offender, Graham, slept for a while on our front room floor of our small terraced house – we also had two young children and three lodgers! He could have benefited from some lessons in personal hygiene, and Jenny used to try to cover the odour with perfume on cotton wool balls stuffed behind the radiators.

Twice Graham disappeared with stuff from our house including Jenny's handbag and my camera. It was a learning time as we realised that our enthusiasm for helping others was no match for the level of brokenness we were encountering. Many years later, however, the very day before we were due to leave Bristol, Graham turned up on our doorstep. He had just returned from Canada where he was regularly involved in church, had been running a YMCA, and had met and married a lovely Christian woman.

It doesn't always end so well! But how good of God to let us know on the eve of our big adventure of moving to Liverpool to plant a new church, that our labour would not be in vain, that what we sowed we would reap. It showed us that though we may never know the outcome of our efforts, God would be faithful to complete what he had started.

Another ex-offender had a dramatic conversion in one of our public meetings. I had introduced him to the church and felt secretly proud of my achievement. All went well for several months. He went into business with one of the young men in the church whom I was pastorally responsible for, and then got engaged to one of the young women. It all seemed too good to be true, and it was. One day he just vanished, leaving a broken heart, outstanding debts and a lot of puzzled people.

We had made two fatal mistakes. The first was never asking him what he was inside for. It turned out that he was a professional con man! The second was that we never compared notes on the stories he was telling us – had we done so, it would have been obvious he was telling us a pack of lies.

The news broke just before one of our public meetings and I had to stand up and explain what had happened. It was humiliating and humbling, but so very important in my character formation. Being conformed to God's image is uncomfortable at least, and downright painful at worst. But it's never destructive, and always liberating when embraced as the Father's loving discipline.

We could do little more than lick our wounds and pray about it. Within 24 hours of reporting the incident, the police made a chance number plate check on a car and caravan in the north east which came up as a stolen vehicle and he was pulled in for questioning. To cut a long story short, he ended up back in prison for the offence. It did not make everything right, but we were comforted that God had heard our prayers and intervened.

God deals with us in many ways, and pride is a big issue for most of us. It was the primary sin of Satan that got him kicked out of heaven (Isaiah 14:12-14). God is very gracious with us and usually does not deal with our pride early on in our journey of faith, but sooner or later it will come up. At this point we have one of two options, to humble ourselves or to be humbled by him (1 Peter 5:5-6). Which would you prefer? I know which I would choose.

I have found that it is good to actually look for opportunities to humble myself; for example being the first to apologise, taking the lower place, and being quick to give others credit. They may all be small things, but they have the effect of crucifying my pride and ensuring that it does not get in the way of God using me. I don't always succeed. A word spoken out of place, in harshness or cynicism, will come back to haunt me very quickly and leave me exposed. It's a sure way to get my repentance and put me back on track.

Jenny and I were on holiday with some good friends – it was the first time we had been away together. I did the washing up, while Geoff sat reading the paper, with seemingly no idea that it might be nice to lend a hand. Eventually my frustration got the better of me and I made a sarcastic comment. Geoff's reply haunts me to this day – "Well, I prefer my laziness to your self-righteousness." Ouch!

We all have our "issues" that God deals patiently with. It may be anger, insecurity, greed, jealousy, unclean thoughts, fear, low self-esteem, comparison, bitterness or apathy. Regardless of the issues that keep us in a state of spiritual immaturity, God will help us. He accepts us as we are, without leaving us as we are. He knows that for each of us there is massive potential that will remain undeveloped if we fail to grow in character. These issues can remain like an iceberg, nine-tenths submerged below the surface, and destroy us when we least expect it, as happened with the Titanic. If we foolishly think we are unsinkable, pride will come before a fall.

When Jesus commanded his followers to go and make disciples (Matthew 28:19), He was telling us to make apprentices. The Greek word for disciple is the word *mathetes*, which means "learner." So we are committed to life-long learning, to remain teachable until the day we die, and to be willing to let others speak life-giving truth into our lives.

Sometimes we are bombarded with a tirade of criticism or anger. To be able to hear and receive the one percent of truth in what they are saying, against the backdrop of the ninety-nine percent of untruth, can be very liberating, and turns a potentially destructive situation into a constructive one. I call it my "one-percent rule." It's all about being a learner from life. Mike Breen's book *A Passionate Life* has an excellent chapter on this. It is his first "lifeshape," the learning circle[1].

Being a learner also means being intentional about getting input to our lives. I have always looked for mentors, and over the years many godly people have honoured me with their insight into my flaws. I remember once expressing frustration about a fellow leader to Phil Vogel, who was at that time providing surgical assistance to my character formation. He simply looked at me and said, "That's just because you aren't getting your own way, Nic." Ouch again! "Wounds from a friend can be trusted" (Proverbs 27:6).

A mentor may not always be available, or even necessary. A lot of what we need is available through what we call "accountable relationships." These are relationships where we have agreed with one or two peers to meet regularly to support and pray for each other, and to ask each other the tough questions.

I believe that being a learner is a lifestyle choice

The kind of questions asked could include: "Have you looked at pornography this week?"; "Have you reacted out of insecurity recently?"; "Is your relationship with God as you want it?"; "Are you loving your wife like Christ loved the church?"; or "What is God telling you to do at the moment, and what are you doing about it?"

We can set a plan of action to deal with current issues and then hold each other to account for doing what we say we will do. These relationships are always by mutual agreement and never imposed. We engage in them because we want to grow in character and in relationship with God. They can be for a season or for many years. Trust and respect are essential if the relationships are going to succeed.

The path of discipleship is always evolving. In the early stages, we are more dependent on the clear advice and instruction of others. Gradually, as we find our feet in our faith, we have a greater need for peer relationships, and as we mature we are able to give to those younger in the faith. And so the cycle of discipleship continues. We never stop learning or growing, because we always remain a disciple.

We make choices to grow because we are looking for the kind of relationship with God that we can take into eternity. We also chose to grow because we want to be of value to the Lord on earth. We know that our ability to serve him will be hampered by a lack of character or a weak relationship with him.

The writer to the Hebrews contrasts those who have fallen away with those who are useful to the Lord. He says, "Land that drinks in the rain often falling on it and that produces a crop useful to those for whom it is farmed receives the blessing of God" (Hebrews 6:7). We receive the refreshing and thirst quenching rain of God's Spirit so that we can be fruitful, not just ornamental.

In the context of spiritual formation and the discipleship journey though, "Being always trumps doing." What he does in us will always be more important than what he does through us. As I said at the start of this chapter, that is a hard message for activists to receive.

I believe that in the discipleship journey, being always trumps doing

In John 15 Jesus speaks of the necessity of pruning. The season of pruning is always a nerve-racking one. Has the plant died? Will it re-grow? Will it ever produce fruit again? But as surely as spring follows winter, the new growth comes and then the blossom, and finally more fruit than you would have believed was possible.

Pruning can be painful, but is necessary for the spiritual growth of churches as well as individuals. Without it, growth is unchecked, size covers underlying ill-health or disease, the growth is not strong and

Imagine if every one of us were involved in a relationship of accountability and committed to spiritual growth

vigorous, and it is ultimately not sustainable. We need to welcome the seasons of pruning, understanding what it means to 'remain or abide in him'. Though little may be happening on the outside, we can trust that on the inside there is valuable preparation going on. Character is being formed, convictions are being refined, and vision is imparted. God is at work.

Returning to Mike Breen's *A Passionate Life*, the semicircle lifeshape is very relevant to this idea of seasons and working with the grain of life, rather than against it.

A soft, teachable heart in church members is a blessing to church leaders. By contrast, I have met many people over the years, who consider themselves God's authority on all things spiritual. They have their own opinion and nothing will change it. Their motto is "I've made up my mind, don't confuse me with the facts." Even if no one agrees with them, it just reinforces their determination to hold those views.

We all need to remember that the seeds of deception are sown in the arrogant attitude that says "I have nothing to learn." Peter says, "Young men, in the same way be submissive to those who are older. All of you, clothe yourselves with humility towards one another, because 'God opposes the proud but gives grace to the humble'" (1 Peter 5:5). As the writer to the Hebrews says, "Obey your leaders and submit to their authority. They keep watch over you as men who must give an account. Obey them so that their work will be a joy, not a burden, for that would be of no advantage to you" (Hebrews 13:17).

Our discipleship journey leads to our being deployed by God, often sooner rather than later. I am always encouraged by God's willingness to take risks with raw new converts. He sees the potential, and is willing to make room for us. He does not mind if we fail, as long as we "fail forward," i.e. we keep moving forward, and are willing to learn from our mistakes.

It is a fallacy that we cannot be used by God until we are mature, or have been to Bible College. Often we are at our most effective when we don't know that it can't be done! New believers can move in levels of faith that more mature Christians have sometimes had knocked out of them. God knows that we can learn more and be changed more quickly in the context of serving and doing, than in the classroom or cloister, because he specialises in on-the-job training. May God give you joy in your learning.

Questions for discussion:

- How is life preparation for eternity?
- Why should we welcome pruning in our lives?
- Would it help you to be accountable to someone for your spiritual growth, and if so, to whom?

Endnotes

1. Breen, M. and Kallestad, W., *A Passionate Life*, (NexGen, 2005)

8. Size matters

So as we progress in individual growth in character and contribution, what is happening to our worshipping, witnessing community? Hopefully it is growing.

Many Christians question whether growth is important. Isn't quality more important than quantity? Isn't it possible to get overly concerned about numbers? Well, yes it is. But God did write a whole book called Numbers in which he was at pains to count everything.

People often point to David's sinful census of the people (1 Chronicles 21), and argue that focusing on numbers angers God. We are told that Satan incited David, presumably by appealing to his pride or insecurity, and certainly if either of those is our motivation, counting numbers will not lead to blessing. We will either become arrogant about our achievements or fearful about our lack of growth. So our motives for wanting to grow must be good ones. What would that look like?

Actually, anything that is alive and healthy will grow: it is a feature of all living things. And if our desire to grow reflects a desire to reach more people with the love of Christ, then it's a motive that God would be pleased with. If it is to have more influence and impact for the Kingdom of God, then it is in line with God's desire for his Kingdom to advance and be the leaven that leavens the whole lump of our society. If it is out of a desire that Jesus would be made famous because of the visibility and credibility that the church gets, then the Father is pleased.

These are good reasons for wanting to grow. It is possible, however, to cross the line into pride and ambition, and God will be quick to expose that.

When we recently tried to discover why we had stopped growing, the Lord put his finger on things, one by one. It was complex: there were leadership issues, structural problems, and undoubtedly some attitudes that God wanted to deal with along the way. The outcome has certainly left us stronger, but more humble. We are much more aware of the grace of God to keep growing the church. Jesus promised to build his church, so it is all about him, not us, but he kindly allows us to work with him in this greatest of all earthly tasks. We are in the bridal preparation business!

I believe that the church is meant to be a sign and a wonder to the world around

God's intends for us to be gathered for impact and scattered for influence. We have a centralised function and a decentralised function. The dynamic of a gathered church creates its own impact, and against the backdrop of declining church attendance, a growing church is visibly bucking the trend. With the generally negative message that comes from the media, most people are under the impression that the church is irrelevant at best and at worst dead. So any report of a church of 1,000 or 2,000 people is a sign. Perhaps even a sign and a wonder.

Thank God for the black majority churches blazing a trail of growth. They are probably the main factor preventing our UK church statistics from looking moribund, especially in London. These churches are generally operating in their own cultural bubble where churchgoing is still much more normal, with those who have recently arrived on UK soil and are seeking like-minded groups for identity and security. These factors all contribute to the dramatic growth in church attendance and new church plants among black communities. But they don't detract from their example and challenge to the white majority churches. May we be provoked to believe God for more!

Before anyone starts to harangue me, I must affirm the great impact and contribution made by many smaller churches. In rural communities, in tough inner-city and sink-estate settings, there are real heroes doing an absolutely amazing job. Churches of thirty, fifty, or one hundred are making waves where they are. Their members are living out sacrificial, incarnational lives that are gradually salting the communities that God has placed them in. For many churches this is God's definition of success, and he is delighted with them.

A big church has the opportunity to make a different kind of impact. Perhaps in a larger town or city, such a church is able to attract the attention of the city and business leaders, the movers and shakers. This in turn brings influence. Perhaps they can cultivate a reputation across the city that makes spreading the gospel easier. A large church comes with the credibility of an organisation that is clearly doing something right. They may be able to put on events that harness the media's power for good.

During the 2010 general election, Frontline was able to attract the attention of politicians of all parties. Cherie Blair visited as part of a trip to Liverpool to see how the church is reaching the marginalised. Nick Clegg held one of his final rallies at the Frontline Centre. David Cameron spent time with two of our church members in particular projects they had pioneered – a social enterprise helping the long-term unemployed, and a mentoring programme working with lads at risk of gun and knife crime.

The local candidates seeking election to be our MP, all gave considerable time to us explaining their views and hearing our concerns. We organised the hustings for the election in our building, with all major parties represented and several of the smaller ones too. The newspapers were keen to report on our engagement with the election build-up.

A large church may well have the resources to do things to a standard of excellence that many seekers today look for in a venue or service. People can be put off by the "It'll do" mentality of many churches today: dowdy decor, hard pews, and cold buildings are not a big turn on. Of course, a friendly welcome takes no physical or financial resource, and indeed, some small churches are better at creating a personal touch for those attending for the first time.

Large gatherings may mislead members into thinking that all the people that God is drawing will come to a church service. The reality is that it takes quite a lot of courage to come to a service, particularly if you have no history of church attendance and have little idea of what to expect. Those who have a church background are more likely to come as a visitor and find God in that context, but many won't.

So we must not just be a "come here" church, but also a "go there" church. Jesus started his ministry with an invitation, "Come, follow me, and I will make you fishers of men" (Matthew 4:19), but his last words were a new command to the disciples, "Go and make disciples of all nations" (Matthew 28:19).

Imagine if our church services were known for their friendliness and inclusiveness

The decentralised function is both individual and collective. As individuals we are to be salt in the world, preserving and bringing flavour to our workplaces, colleges, schools and neighbourhoods. We are sent as ambassadors of Christ (2 Corinthians 5:20). We are the sons of the kingdom sown into the world (Matthew 13:37-38) to bring the values of goodness, kindness, truthfulness and love to those around us, to produce a harvest of souls, to extend the Kingdom of God. We are all missionaries wherever we spend the bulk of our time, being the good news of Jesus, and speaking when the opportunity arises. As St Francis of Assisi is credited with saying, "Preach the gospel at all times, and if necessary use words."

John, a GP, regularly prayed for his patients when the opportunity arose. Giving them a big hug was also part of his therapy at times. He risked being misunderstood, even having a formal complaint made against him, but the many patients who got touched by God, and some who came to faith, were a prize worth risking his reputation for. John seemed to have particular faith to pray for people bound up with fear. Authoritative prayers of deliverance gave several patients dramatic breakthroughs. Some who had suffered terrible abuse or traumas were wonderfully set free, amazed that what psychotherapy or drugs had failed to do, God had done in a moment. This is being salt and light in the workplace.

There are many who need a listening ear, who have troubles, or who just want to talk about themselves. You just need to ask the right questions, be genuine and show the love of God. Jenny, my wife, volunteers for an organisation that supports young mums who are overwhelmed with the pressures of young children, by loving them and giving practical support ironing, shopping, and child-minding. She has been able to speak God's truth, signpost one couple to Christian counselling, and invite one woman to church who then gave her life to Jesus.

It's not rocket science, as Heidi Baker says, it's just "loving the one in front of you."[1] May God give us eyes to see the opportunities to show his love, and the confidence to speak when the time comes.

The decentralised influence also occurs through small groups. The early church met not only in the temple courts as a large congregation, but also in homes (Acts 2:46). Many of Paul's letters were written to the church in a city or region, but also to the church in a particular house, for example Prisca and Aquila's house, Nympha's house, and Archippus' house (Romans 16:3-5, Colossians 4:15, and Philemon 1:2). These mid-sized communities or extended households of perhaps ten, twenty, thirty or more people were the backbone of the church and allowed it to spread its influence across a city with minimal infrastructure.

The early church clearly did have organisation and structure as the gospel spread rapidly. The apostles' teaching was the under-girding, stabilising influence to those who were daily coming to faith (Acts 2:42). The distribution of the proceeds of land and property sales to meet the needs of the poor was overseen by the apostles (Acts 4:34-35). Seeing to the needs of the widows was delegated to the seven deacons, while the apostles kept their focus on prayer and teaching (Acts 6:1-6). They appear to have met regularly both in the temple forecourts and in homes.

It's unrealistic to expect an emerging organic church to require no organisation or administration. If it has no structure it cannot grow beyond a certain size, because anything that grows has to have an infrastructure to support the growth. The body of Christ is not like an amoeba!

The human body has an amazing infrastructure which allows it to grow and function for many decades. A body without a skeleton would just be a skin sack full of organs in a pool on the floor. A body without a nerve communication system would fail to operate. We

Imagine if we all committed to "loving the one in front of us."

must welcome structure that is for our benefit and allows us to keep growing.

But structures must not become a sacred cow that cannot be touched. If a structure starts to hinder, it must be changed, or we become slaves to what we have created. Our structures need to be flexible like a wineskin, to serve the new things that God will do. There must be diverse opportunities for the expression and development of gifts. There needs to be a variety of vehicles to allow the gospel to reach every man, woman and child.

Growth creates challenges because it becomes impossible for any one person to know every other person. We must find other ways of providing that sense of community where we are known fully and can know others fully. A church service may leave some feeling isolated or overwhelmed if other church members are not intentionally looking out for them.

In a large church it can be harder for members to see a direct relationship between the money they give and the activities that go on. As an increasingly professional staff body emerges, some may feel that they no longer need to volunteer to make things happen, or if they do volunteer, that they are less valued. It is more difficult for people to feel connected to the senior leaders. The complex administration of a growing church can seem more like a business than a body to some. Bureaucracy increases, and people can feel they are being blocked by red tape from doing things that used to require just a nod from the pastor. A large church can also make other churches feel insecure, threatened or not needed.

All of these are real but not insurmountable problems. The prize that makes it worthwhile is the emergence of the church that Jesus died for and is coming back for, a church that can be the head and not the tail (Deuteronomy 28:13), a church that threatens the very culture of our fallen world, a church that can resource city-transforming activities (more of that later), a church that the gates of hell will not prevail against, a church that can reflect the breadth of the Ephesians 4:11-13 ministry gifts, and a church that is visible to the whole city like a light on the hill pointing the way to Jesus.

A large growing church does not necessarily have to meet all in one place. The multi-site church movement in the USA is a healthy challenge to that assumption. It can have high visibility and city-wide impact because of its strong single identity, common leadership and coordinated programme. It avoids the fragmentation that resulted from the new churches' congregational model in the UK during the 1980s, when the autonomy of those congregations tended to lead to either impotence or independence. In the latter case, the congregation eventually pulled away to form its own church. Impact was usually lost, and the church either became increasingly irrelevant or began its own quest to be the big fish in the pond. However, the seeds of self-destruction were usually not far below the surface.

Over the years we have worked hard to build relationships with other church leaders. We have a strong commitment to the city-wide church. In scripture the churches in the city, for example at Ephesus or in Corinth, were the only large structures that were known. We clearly can't turn the clock back to achieve that singleness of structure, but we can work towards a unity of spirit and level of cooperation that allows the church to have a united witness.

In Liverpool in 1998, John Cavanagh and I formed "Together for the harvest" to bring together the evangelical churches in the Liverpool city region. Over the years hundreds of leaders have worked together across the region on specific projects, and the mistrust of the past has largely been replaced with great cooperation. I believe that there is only one church here, made up of many congregations. When I ask our people, "How many churches are there in Liverpool?" the united response is, "There is one church in Liverpool." May we continue to grow in love and unity for the sake of the gospel.

Imagine if everyone took the time to introduce themselves to one person they didn't know at every church service

Size does matter, and God is interested in building many multi-thousand member churches in our cities. Let's not run away from the challenges and revert to what we know is safe and secure. Let's believe and work for something that is bigger than any of us have yet experienced. Let's trust God to figure out how to do it as we go.

Questions for discussion:

- How can we avoid "playing the numbers game"?
- Why is size important to God?
- What aspects of the centralised and decentralised church do you value?

Endnotes

1. Heidi and Rolland Baker head up Iris Ministries (www.irismin.org) and have worked extensively in Mozambique. Her books *Always Enough* (Chosen Books, 2003) and *Compelled by Love* (Charisma House, 2008) exemplify her motto of "loving the one in front of you."

9. The leadership factor

I was wandering aimlessly through the school courtyard at the age of fourteen. I had never thought of myself as a leader, despite being captain of the rugby team for three years. Being short, I had some self-image issues to deal with (but that's another story). My biology teacher, who ran the youth group that had changed my life two years earlier, approached me and started chatting. He remarked, "You know, you are a leader, Nic." It was a totally alien concept to me, but the seed was sown and as the years went by the label felt more comfortable.

"No leadership, no future," said one of my mentors from the past, Dwight Smith. I believe in leadership. I believe it is one of the most important and yet neglected dimensions of many churches. It is rarely taught at theological colleges or Bible schools, though that situation is improving.

Leadership, according to John Maxwell, is influence. As such, it is something that we can all have. All of us have the opportunity to influence the human beings we are in contact with, either for good or evil. We can either acknowledge our influence or deny its existence. We can run from it, or welcome it like a friend.

I believe in leadership

When Jenny and I moved to a new area in Bristol, we had been married for three years and our family was growing. We part-owned a house with two other couples and a single guy, but it was time to try and buy one of our own. We decided to move to an area of cheaper housing, knowing that with our church emphasis on community, others would follow suit. It was also an ideal opportunity to start a new congregation.

We found a delightful little terraced house, and set up home. Sure enough, others started to move into the neighbourhood. Having already been running one of the small groups, I was convinced that I was the right person to lead this emerging community. Neil, who was responsible for the church in our part of town, came for a chat, which I assumed was to invite me to head up this new congregation. He let me down gently in his best pastoral fashion, and to say I was surprised would be an understatement.

I had to choose between going off in a sulk and "taking my ball away," or reacting with some maturity. In the end I chose to do something quite counter-intuitive. I decided to take as much initiative as I possibly could to help grow the congregation without the title of leader. Oh, how I long for people like that in church now.

I started a decorating team. As a way of getting to know the neighbours and blessing the neighbourhood, we offered to help the elderly local residents with their decorating and other practical needs.

Imagine if we all took the initiative and responsibility of leadership without having to have the title

We had a great time, and other initiatives followed. I discovered that not being the official leader was actually quite liberating. It also taught me that you don't need the title to actually lead.

Less than a year later, the then leader of the congregation stepped down and I was asked to take over. The congregation grew within a few years to about 80 people.

God always uses leaders to get things done. On the macro-biblical scale we see great leaders like Abraham, Moses, Deborah, David, Esther and Elijah, who changed history and the destiny of nations. We also see those who made less of a splash on the pages of the Bible, like Nympha who had a church in her house, like the heroes of Hebrews 11:35-40 who endured great hardship and didn't even get their names recorded, and like the servant girl who introduced Naaman to Elisha, resulting in his healing (2 Kings 5:2-5). All had influence in their sphere; all exercised leadership.

In the church context the Bible describes many types of leadership roles. There are elders and deacons; there are apostles, prophets, evangelists, pastors and teachers; there are overseers and under-shepherds; there are those who "stand before" or lead (*proistemi* in the Greek, Romans 12:8) and there are those who pilot or steer, govern or administrate (*kubernesis* in the Greek, 1 Corinthians 12:28).

Church leaders are often maligned and misunderstood, and they do sometimes get it wrong. There are many pitfalls along the way to be avoided for the leader to be of use to God and blessing to the church. Most leaders have considerable drive and ambition, but it's not a career you chose for social advancement, for a high-flying salary or for the pension perks. So there has to be a real call of God to keep going. For anyone called to a significant position of leadership, there should be a government warning on the packet: "This occupation may seriously damage your health and wealth." Giving up my job as a GP in 1986 certainly did the latter, and to be honest, I think it has also taken its toll on the former

The pitfalls of pride, secret sin, marriage tensions, sexual temptation, discouragement, anger and depression all lie in wait to consume the unsuspecting leader. Insecurities, fear of the opinion of the people, and gaining significance from being needed, are other threats.

This is why any leader needs a support network of people who love them, who can speak the truth in love to them and call them to account for their actions. Such accountability should be welcomed. It is not a threat if we are secure in our calling; it is a vital safeguard against the schemes of the enemy. Although there should be formal structures for such accountability, informal, relationally-based accountability will usually be more effective.

At a John Wimber conference in the 1980s, I spent time with the wife of one of the couples that Jenny and I were friendly with and had discipled. I was not aware of anything untoward, or inappropriate, but the wife of the senior leader saw us chatting and it rang her alarm bells. A week or so later she confronted me and told me to take care. At the time I would have denied that there was any danger, but looking back I think it was a timely warning that prevented any potential marital problems, for the other lady or for me.

So why does anyone subject themselves to the perils of leadership? Surely it is for the prize of seeing Jesus build his church, to see the church make herself ready for his return, and to be able to anticipate the Master say, "Well done, good and faithful servant. You have been faithful over a little; I will set you over much. Enter into the joy of your master!" (Matthew 25:21). To share in the Father's joy is an amazing idea. As Paul said, "We make it our aim to please him" (2 Corinthians 5:9).

So how do you know if someone is a leader? Look to see if anyone is following him or her. As the saying goes, "If anyone calls himself a leader, but has no-one following him, he is just a man taking a walk." There are many different styles of the leadership gift, but the ability to inspire others to follow is at the heart of it. Leaders must see or sense where God is leading, and be able to point the way to others.

The leader's life must be one of integrity. They must be utterly trustworthy. Trust is a commodity that is hard-earned, but is easily lost, and very difficult to rebuild when it is broken. A leader's words and lifestyle will constantly be under scrutiny. Things that others seem to get away with, with impunity, can destroy a leader's reputation.

I have found over the years that the slightest exaggeration, the smallest white lie, the hint of a cutting or cynical remark come back to haunt me so quickly. The tongue is truly hard to tame, but for the sake of those who follow, tame it we must.

I believe that every leader will go through a "death to ambition" experience at some point, and often at many points

God's preparation of a leader is usually a bumpy ride. Because leaders have the ability to affect the lives of so many others for good or ill, the Lord is at pains to prepare the character and heart of the leader. Failure, being misunderstood, false accusation, lack of appreciation, frustrating circumstances and delays are all used by God to speed up the process of death that has to work in us.

As Paul says, "Death is at work in us, but life is at work in you" (2 Corinthians 4:12).

We emerge from the fire with our call intact, but our self-sufficiency ruined forever. We are like Jacob who wrestled with the angel of the Lord. We walk with a permanent limp, a reminder of our encounter with him (Genesis 32:25). Our natural strength must be broken if God is to use us and we are not to burn out or blow up.

Leaving Bristol was an exhilarating experience, but also a devastating one. The year before we decided to leave was a "dark year of the soul," and I knew that something had to change. The vision to see the church turned inside out was not going to happen the way I longed for it. Despite giving up my medical practice and running a full-time evangelism team for five years, the church seemed as entrenched as ever in an inward mind-set. Looking back, I'm sure that I was proud and judgemental, but as we considered the future, the only way forward seemed to be outside of the church that Jenny and I had loved and given everything to. It was a painful blow, and deeply affected both Jenny and me. In all of our pain we realised that if we were to be blessed in any new venture then it was essential that we left with the leaders' blessing.

So we prayed . . . and prayed. It felt like someone had turned the lights out and I didn't know where the switch was. The only flicker of light I had was a verse in Habakkuk: "The vision is yet for the appointed time; it hastens toward the goal, and it will not fail. Though it tarries, wait for it; it will certainly come, it will not delay" (Habakkuk 2:3, NASB). And so we waited. I had always had such certainty about being in the right place at the right time doing the right thing, but this was something else. After six months of waiting and praying, the floodlights all came on at once and God spoke. Liverpool!

The leaders graciously allowed us to recruit an awesome team and the rest is history, but it was with a limp that we made the journey north.

Fortunately these "breaking" experiences do not come all at once. If anything they seem to come in cycles, with a deepening of the process each time round. We start with a little humbling in the early stages, but progress to a fuller surrender as time goes on. We are convicted of more obvious sins at the beginning, but later on our hearts come under more searching scrutiny from the Holy Spirit. Subtle attitudes that need changing are exposed. These are usually heart issues that others may not even be aware of.

God is committed to making us more like Jesus in our leadership. If others are going to model themselves on us, we had better be sure that we are modelling ourselves on Jesus. Then we can say like Paul, "Follow my example, as I follow the example of Christ" (1 Corinthians 11:1).

It's not a case of waiting till you are perfect before God can use you. God will use you from day one. In fact, some of your early experiences will be the most formative of your future leadership. We all learn by doing, and we learn more from failure than success.

Leaders are no more important to God than anyone else, but their particular gift to the body of Christ does require others to respond to it if it is going to function well. Other gifts can operate to some extent independently of other people's cooperation, but not leadership.

Leaders need the agreement of others to lead, and usually people just vote with their feet if they do not want to be led. Yet it's in the nature of leaders to lead, and if that desire is constantly thwarted, the impulse will turn inward in frustration and become self-destructive, resulting in bitterness and anger. It will implode or explode; neither are pretty sights.

Authority is a precious commodity and must not be used as a means to get our own way. It is a sacred trust from those who are being led to those who are leading which must never be abused. Otherwise it will cause tremendous damage both to the individual and to the

Imagine if every leader was set free from pride and insecurity

body of Christ as a whole. Although leadership cannot operate well in a democracy, without a consensus of support, it will not work. Authority is like a bar of soap: the more you have to use it, the less you have got. Leadership is to serve, not to lord it over others – Jesus made that quite clear (Matthew 20:28).

I believe that authority can never be taken; it must always be given

When leaders pull rank to get their way in a particular situation, it looks ugly. It's like a parent whose default when dealing with their toddler is to shout, "Do it because I said so!"

There are many sources of authority in leadership. There is the authority of position, but if we have to rely on it we have missed the point. There is the authority of our expertise or knowledge. If you call in a plumber and he says you need a new thermostat, you generally accept his advice because he should know what he is talking about.

There is the authority of spiritual gifting and anointing. We accept the authority of the prophet because we want to hear from God, and we accept the authority of the person with the gift of healing because we want to be healed. We submit to these people because they are God's gift to us. Leadership is a spiritual gift as well as a natural one. When we recognise it, let's benefit from it by submitting to it. Submission is of course a heart attitude, not blind obedience.

The greatest authority however comes from our character, our integrity and our trustworthiness. If we do not have integrity written through us, like the words in a stick of rock, then we will not be trusted for long. We may be able to fool some with our charismatic personality, our eloquent oration, or even our spiritual giftedness for a short period of time, but our true character will always come out in the end.

Lack of integrity causes such a loss of honour for the church at large, let alone the specific congregation that is affected. We need men and women of proven character to lead. The qualifications for elders and deacons in the pastoral epistles of Timothy and Titus (1 Timothy 3:1-14 and Titus 1:5-9), with the exception of the ability to teach, are all to do with character.

Many unfortunately lead for the wrong reasons, like the need to be needed, the desire for recognition, the adrenalin of power, the desire to control, or the love of being centre stage. The combination of pride and insecurity in a leader is a toxic mix that spells disaster for the leader and the led. If our actions don't result from genuinely wanting the best for those we are leading and a desire to serve and please God, there is still much work to do on our heart.

Many years ago when I gently confronted a fellow leader about his insecure reaction to something, I was shocked by the outburst that followed. It was a public place, and he exploded loudly, "I AM NOT INSECURE!" It was a bit of a giveaway.

Many great and godly leaders are serving God and doing

I believe that pride and insecurity are the most common and lethal weaknesses in a leader

I believe that servant leaders should be honoured, supported, rewarded, and protected

their best for others. An honest and loving heart does not, however, ensure a bump-free ride. Even the church can be an establishment that wounds its leaders and then shoots the wounded. I have met so many leaders carrying emotional injuries from angry, immature, jealous or offended church members or co-leaders.

It is one of the great travesties of church life that those who give their lives to serve others through leadership can be unappreciated and carry painful wounds from the actions, words or attitudes of other Christians. May God deliver us from the squabbles and conflicts that afflict the body of Christ.

With so much at stake, it is easy to see why some are reluctant to step up into leadership. When we have been hurt or taken advantage of, it is all too easy to retreat into safety zones. After Jesus' death Peter went back to the familiarity and comfort of fishing, thinking, "Here's something I know I can do." What will we do with our gift, hide it under a bushel? Or use it to serve the church and advance the kingdom?

Christian leadership must not be confined to the church. It is needed in business, education, the arts and media, in health care and social services. Influence is the key. We need prophets in the media, apostles in business, evangelists in sales, pastors in human resources and teachers in education and training, to name but a few.

Leadership is a gift that grows. Jenny and I got our first taste of it in 1973 when we were asked to lead the Christian Union group in our halls of residence in Bristol. I cringe when I think of our combined ignorance and immaturity. But God was there and saw to it that we did not do too much damage and learned valuable lessons along the way. It's a little-known

I believe that God has given leadership gifts for the marketplace as well as for ministry

fact that I led worship on guitar for a year – when no one else can play, anyone can be an expert!

In those days I would tend to be overly "spiritual" and fail to use common sense or draw on the wisdom of other older, more mature Christians – so common in young leaders. I think God just looks down from heaven and smiles, loving the fact that we are having a go even if we are clueless! He must promptly dispatch his angels to cover our mistakes.

I thank God for other leaders around me who encouraged me. The leaders in the church in Bristol gave me opportunities to lead small groups, start congregations, join the main leadership team of the church and eventually become an elder leading a full-time evangelism training team. When we prove faithful with the small things, God will entrust us with greater things, as Jesus said in the parable of the talents (Matthew 25:19-23).

It's always good to look for opportunities to take responsibility, rather than to wait to be given authority. My first responsibility in the church in Bristol was to organise lifts to the meetings for those who did not have transport. I managed it for all of one week, and then lost interest. I have often wondered how the man who led the group, Dave Day, was so patient with me.

There is no such thing as a failure, only a learning experience. If God was an examination board, there would be no failures, just plenty of re-sits! He is so committed to our learning and transformation that he will not allow us to bypass any critical stage in our development. If we find ourselves coming up against the same set of difficult circumstance again and again, it's probably worth asking, "Is there something that I am not hearing or learning here?"

There are clearly levels of leadership, just as there are levels of maturity, anointing and experience. In his book *Good to Great*[1], Jim Collins talks about a Level Five leader. Such a person has the vision and courage to lead and is defined by their professional will and personal humility. The best leaders are not necessarily the most impressive or the most eloquent, but more often those with a steely resolve combined with a quiet humble authority.

Jesus was a classic Level Five leader. You don't find him bragging about his achievements, or quickly agreeing to others' opinions that he was the Messiah. If Jesus was moulded by today's western culture, he would have put a full ad in the national newspapers announcing his arrival, his miracles would be documented by CNN and distributed to all media outlets, and he would have had his own website – messiah.com. In-depth interviews with Jeremy Paxman and a revealing life history documentary with Piers Morgan would follow to ensure people got the message.

In fact, when Isaiah prophesies about the coming Christ, he says that "He had no beauty or majesty to attract us to him, nothing in his

Imagine if all of our leaders were characterised by great determination, with equal humility and integrity

appearance that we should desire him" (Isaiah 53:2-3). At times he seemed to deliberately put people off from following him. This is so different from the celebrity culture which does sometimes creep into the church.

God does not choose the beautiful people to lead, he chooses those whose hearts are hungry for him, who are willing to shoulder the responsibility for others, and who are gripped by the dream of what could be. He chooses those who are humble and teachable, and walk with a limp. He chooses the "foolish things of the world to shame the wise . . . the weak things of the world to shame the strong" (1 Corinthians 1:27).

Women in leadership? Of course. Why rob yourself of some of the most gifted leaders on the planet? As William Booth, founder of the Salvation Army used to say, "All my best men are women!" We only have to look at some of the great women of the Bible like Deborah, Esther, Mary, Priscilla, and those nameless ones in Hebrews, "women received back their dead, raised to life again. Others were tortured and refused to be released, so that they might gain a better resurrection" (Hebrews 11:35)

Our problems with women in leadership can be contextual: understanding the historical and cultural context of the Scriptures that appear to put limits on women's ministry. Or they can link to our upbringing or personal prejudice. For a fuller exploration of this subject I recommend either *Why Not Women* by Loren Cunningham and David Hamilton[2] or *The Turning Tide* by Brenda Robson[3].

Questions for discussion:

- Who is your favourite biblical leader and why?

- In what context have you experienced a measure of leadership? (Remember leadership is influence.)

- Do you see any limits on the roles that a women can play in leadership, and if so, why?

Endnotes

1. Collins, J., *Good to Great*, (Random House, 2001)

2. Cunningham, L. and Hamilton D, *Why not women: A Biblical Study of Women in Missions, Ministry, and Leadership*, (YWAM Publishing, 2000)

3. Robson, B., *The Turning Tide*, (Harper Collins, 1989)

10. The ministry gifts

Leadership is usually characterised by one or more of the Ephesians 4 ministry gifts – the apostle, prophet, evangelist, pastor, and teacher (Ephesians 4:11-13). I view these more as descriptions than positions in leadership. There are many ideas about how these gifts function, but let's have a look at some of them.

The Apostle

The apostle is one who builds the church. Paul described himself as an "expert builder," using the Greek word *architekton* from which we get the word architect (1 Corinthians 3:10). Jesus said "I will build my church" (Matthew 16:18) and he is our apostle and high priest (Hebrews 3:1), but he does it with the cooperation of human agencies. God wants to do everything through his people; we are his fellow workers (2 Corinthians 6:1). The apostle is one who pioneers and breaks new ground to plant churches.

The word apostle means "a sent one." Jesus was a "sent one" and the root of the word apostle, is seen in John 3:16: "For God so loved the world that he *sent* his one and only son." So theoretically even a short-term mission is an apostolic venture.

The apostle as the *architekton* has a blueprint or plan in mind, as God gifts them to see the overall shape and form of what He is building. They are able to coordinate the work of other ministry gifts so that the body can build itself up in love. They must then be a visionary and "big-picture" person.

It is normal for those who are sent to operate in signs and wonders. Jesus said "Go into all the world and preach the good news to all creation...and these signs will accompany those who believe: In my name they will cast out demons; they will speak in new tongues . . . they will place their hands on sick people, and they will get well" (Mark 16:16-18).

When Paul's apostleship was called into question by the Corinthians, he said, "You are the seal of my apostleship" (1 Corinthians 9:2, NASB). In other words, the proof of his apostolic calling was the church that he had planted in Corinth.

The apostle is placed at the head of the list of ministry gifts, not only in Ephesians 4 but also in 1 Corinthians 12:28, where Paul says that "In the church God has appointed first of all apostles, second prophets . . ." This does not mean that apostles are more important than others, but they are usually the first on the scene, and set the tone and direction for what takes place. They

I believe that the apostle's primary calling is to plant and build churches

are concerned with the whole building, whereas other gifts may be more focused on one specific area. The apostle may well have other gifts from the list that further equip them for their role. These secondary gifts, plus the personality and temperament of the apostle, means there are as many varieties of apostles as there are people with that calling.

The Prophet

The prophet is the eagle eye, hovering over the scene to see what God is doing. Prophets have unique insights for specific areas of church life at particular times. They normally operate in the spiritual gift of prophecy, which means they are involved in exhorting/challenging, edifying/strengthening and consoling/reassuring the church (1 Corinthians 14:3). It has been said that prophecy is to stir up, build up and cheer up the church. The prophet will work closely with the apostle in a foundational role in the church (Ephesians 2:20), and together they make a good team: one with the big picture, the other with specific insights and revelations.

In some ways the prophet performs quality control on a building site. They are often able to put their finger on things when others are still groping around in the dark looking for an answer to a problem. They will smell sin in the camp from a mile away, and may be inclined to declare Old Testament-style fire and brimstone messages. They need a massive dose of grace and patience to counteract this tendency.

The prophet may tend to only have one time frame – now. So if a word is not acted on immediately, they can feel frustrated and think it has been ignored. They need to discern between a word that God is bringing to them personally, and a word for the church, as well as when a word is for delivering, or simply for praying over. When God introduces Abraham as a prophet to Abimelech, Abimelech is told

I believe in apostles and prophets

that Abraham will pray for him. Significantly, this is the first mention of a prophet in the Bible, and the result of Abraham's prayers is a healing miracle (Genesis 20:7, 17). When military commanders speak to Jeremiah the prophet, they ask him to pray for them (Jeremiah 42:2). There is a strong link between the prophetic ministry and intercession.

Both apostles and prophets are likely to preach and teach, but because of the prophets' gift of exhortation, they are likely to operate in more of a preaching than teaching style.

The Pastor

The role of the pastor, which is the same word as "shepherd" in the Greek – *poimen*, is described in Zechariah chapter 11:16. Although the context is obscure, the Lord describes a bad shepherd by the things he will fail to do, and therefore implies what a good shepherd should be doing.

He names four roles: (NASB)

1. "To care for the perishing." This is a clear indication that the pastor should be concerned for the lost as well as the found. I have met many pastors who have become preoccupied with the saved, and have lost sight of the lost.

2. "To seek the scattered." This speaks of the backslidden, those who once believed and may still believe, but have got disconnected from other Christians. Many have lost their way because of life's difficult circumstances, some because of being treated badly by church; others were never birthed properly into the kingdom and

lacked the strength to survive the early days of spiritual life. Whatever the reason, the Father wants to reach out to them. We need to seek out the backslidden, as well as pray for them.

3. "To heal the broken." This is more familiar pastoral territory! So many are drawn to Christ because of their brokenness and see in him the answer to their need. The pastor will naturally want to care for the broken. Motivated by compassion, and with a love for people, there is a tendency for pastors to try to meet needs single-handedly, thus unwittingly raising expectations they cannot meet. Pastors can easily be overwhelmed by demands and have to ensure the load is shared by other carers and counsellors.

I believe that every pastor needs a healthy mix of compassion for the lost, and concern for the believer's wellbeing

4. "To sustain the one standing." Here we can see that after all the needs of the previous three groups, there are at last some who are "still standing." Phew! These are regular people who just want to be loved, encouraged, taught, equipped, and used in some way that harnesses their gifts.

So in essence, the pastor is the shepherd of the sheep. They care for and protect the flock, and go after the strays. Usually moved by compassion, as Jesus was (Matthew 20:34), they are the glue that holds the local church together. They are likely to be more merciful than the prophet, who tends to see things in black and white, and more compassionate than the apostle, who is likely to be more strategically focused.

All ministries are to build up others (Ephesians 4:12), and the pastor must ensure that structures for nurturing are developed so that everyone is cared for, no matter how large the church gets. Pastors are likely to have a strong fatherly or motherly instinct for new spiritual babies and make provision for them. They will administer discipline to the flock but loathe having to punish, like any good parent.

The Teacher

The teacher is concerned for the truth of the Bible to be communicated and applied to every member of the church. Teachers are concerned for a high level of biblical literacy, and should be able to inspire members to feed themselves from God's word. They will study to be sure that they are free from error, and will guard the church from theological deception. Teachers, with their love of structure and order, can at times miss the flow of the Spirit. They need the other gifts to connect them to what the Holy Spirit is doing at a specific moment in time.

The Evangelist

Evangelists are of course passionate about one thing – souls. The urgency of reaching the lost is their primary concern, and they don't know why the rest of the church does not see things as they do. Like prophets, evangelists are prone to frustration, but with what they perceive as self-centred and lazy saints. They can fall into self-righteousness and condemn the church for its lack of outward focus.

Imagine the church being so fully equipped with ministry gifts that it reached the "full and complete standard of Christ"

(Ephesians 4:11-13)

However, their passion is infectious and a vital ingredient to the body. They are needed to equip the saints for the critical function of reaching the least, the last and the lost. They need to see themselves as part of a team, and not a lone ranger, or saviour of the world – we already have one!

According to Ephesians 4:12, the primary role of ministries is to "prepare God's people for works of service, so that the body of Christ may be built up." This needs to be in all three dimensions of up, in and out. In the local church, these ministries will help raise others into ministry and leadership. They are vital to the body of Christ coming to maturity, and will operate "until we all reach unity in the faith and in the knowledge of the Son of God and become mature, attaining to the whole measure of the fullness of Christ" (Ephesians 4:13) In other words, they are needed until we are prepared for Christ's return.

These ministry gifts shouldn't be confined within one local church. In their mature expression they are gifts to the whole body of Christ, and should be released to bless other local churches, the citywide expression of the church, or further afield. We have seen that with several leaders in Frontline.

At every level of leadership, whether people are leading a small group, a worship team, a course, a ministry, a community, or a church, there should be elements of these gifts and motivations at work. Bearing in mind these roles are more descriptive than prescriptive there is an endless variety of expression, so there is no need to feel boxed in by labels. The advantage of gaining insight to our primary ministry role is to learn how to operate in teams and complement each other.

I believe leadership is plural

Leadership is always plural. Jesus himself was not alone, as he only did the things he saw the Father doing. He sent his disciples out two as a time, and appointed elders (plural) to lead in the church. Paul went out with Barnabas and then Timothy to plant churches, and always had a team around him. We need to always be looking for the people with whom God is placing us. Sometimes we may be team leaders and other times we lead from within a team. Leadership can be a lonely place and we need others around us just to survive.

Dave Connolly and I would not necessarily recommend our co-equal type of leadership for every local church setting, yet this is how God has led and blessed us. I am grateful to God for giving me Dave to lead with, though it's not always been an easy journey as we are so different and both quite stubborn. But I have always appreciated the support and love that has been there for me whenever I have needed it. Genesis 2:18 says that it is not good for man to be alone. It wasn't then, and it isn't now.

I think we both operate in a mixture of ministry gifts. When Dave travels to other churches he is functioning apostolically, and when I bring vision to the church I am acting prophetically. However, Dave normally functions in the prophetic and pastoral, and I in apostolic and teaching ministries. Neither of us are evangelists, but we are both passionate about reaching the lost. Our first twenty years of working together has been a pleasure, as well as means of sanctification.

Questions for discussion:

- How do Ephesians 4 ministry gifts equip the local church?
- Which of the Ephesians 4 ministry gifts do you most identify with and why?
- What have you found to be the challenge of working in teams?

11. The transformational agenda

In different parts of the world and at different times in history, the gospel has had a truly transformational effect. Whole towns, cities and even nations have been changed. It's almost as though the kingdom of God has come prematurely in its fullness. Crime has drastically reduced, marriages have been mended, communities have been reconciled, healing and health has been the norm, economies have prospered and the church has been elevated to pride of place in the civic context.

One young couple whose lives had been devastated by addiction and whose child had been taken into care ended up in a hostel for the homeless. After encountering the gospel through an Alpha course, they started coming to church. They came off the drugs and gradually rebuilt their lives. I had the privilege of marrying them and watching them make a great home for their children – the one who was in care as well as two gorgeous new ones. A city is transformed one life at a time.

When we moved to Liverpool in 1991, it felt like downtown Beirut. On many nights joy riders were tearing up the tarmac outside our house, and the fire brigade was frequently called to derelict houses being set on fire by the local youth. Police helicopters were overhead looking for crime suspects. On one occasion they warned local residents through a loudspeaker system about stolen drums of toxic chemicals that might have been abandoned in the neighbourhood. Cars left on the road were regularly broken into or vandalised.

In 1991 the city had rotting piles of rubbish in every street and back alley and rats were having a heyday due to a long-running rubbish collectors' strike. The day we moved into our house was the 28th June, the day that the strike was finally called off. It felt like a prophetic indication that God would allow us to make a difference, and that we would see the city transformed.

Over the next few years other Christians moved into the street. Derelict houses were bought and renovated, and local residents were impacted by the gospel. The street soon became a very desirable area to live in. The local media even talked about the "gentrification of Wavertree." I'm not sure I would go that far, but the impact was tangible.

There are many Old Testament Scriptures that set a biblical precedent. Isaiah 58:12 says that the righteous will "rebuild ancient ruins," "raise up age-old foundations," and be called "Repairer of Broken Walls" and "Restorer of Streets with Dwellings." Isaiah 60:1-10 refers to our light coming and the glory of the Lord rising upon us, the wealth of the nations coming to us, foreigners building up our walls, and kings ministering to us. It adds, "I will make peace your governor and righteousness your ruler" (Isaiah 60:17).

We can view these Scriptures in the light of the immediate circumstances of Israel in her exile and restoration, as well as seeing them as descriptions of the heavenly kingdom after Christ's return.

But the kingdom has been breaking in ever since Christ's first coming, and will continue to do so until we see its fullness when Jesus comes again. So we can expect some of these glorious descriptions to apply to this current church age, as certain times and places become a window on the future.

I believe that the gospel has the power to transform not only the individual, but whole communities, cities and nations

Does it happen in Scripture? The preaching of Jonah had a dramatic impact on Nineveh (Jonah 3:4-6). Jerusalem was the first city to see the church's impact, and although the whole of its population was not transformed, in Acts 5:28, the disciples were accused of having "filled Jerusalem with their teaching." There was clearly a saturation effect.

Later on, when the campaign in Ephesus took place, we see an interesting progression. First of all Paul found men of peace (Luke 10:6), who are simply called disciples in Acts 19. They became his beach-head in the city and from there he preached the gospel more widely. After that he began a more intensive phase of disciple making in the school of Tyrannus. Signs and wonders took place, demons were cast out, and as occult powers were challenged, many disclosed their magic practices and burned their magic books. The value of those articles was around five million pounds in today's money – imagine what impact that had on the occult economy.

All this was followed by a backlash. Demetrius, a silversmith who made silver shrines to the local goddess Artemis complained about the loss of income due to so many people becoming believers. He stirred up all the other craftsmen involved in similar trades and soon there was a full-scale riot. Amidst the uproar Demetrius protested, that the goddess "will be robbed of her divine majesty." Clearly the gospel was having an impact not only on the seen world of people, money and places, but also on the unseen world of spiritual powers that Paul wrote about later to the Ephesian church (Ephesians 6:12).

Every level of life in the city was being affected. Luke says, "This went on for two years, so that all the Jews and Greeks who lived in the province of Asia [modern-day western Turkey] heard the word of the Lord (Acts 19:10). It was no overnight sensation, but made an impact across the whole region.

Throughout history when the church has been at its best or there has been a sovereign move of God, not only have countless people been saved, but the knock-on effect has been transformation of the town, city or nation.

Loren Cunningham has documented much of this in his book *The Book that Transforms Nations*[1]. He gives the example of Norway, a nation that has the highest standard of living in the world – yet it was not always so.

Hans Nielsen Hauge was a simple Norwegian farmer who lived from 1771-1824. Although from a God-honouring family, he didn't become a Christian until he was 25. The country at that time was immensely poor and subject to its neighbouring countries. People weren't allowed to travel or meet publicly without government permission, yet Hauge felt compelled to travel everywhere on foot and on skis to preach the good news. He and other leaders he raised up were jailed on many occasions. He distributed Bibles wherever he went and started 1,000 home-based groups within the state church, in a total population of only 800,000. As they studied the Bible, prayed and lived out what they were reading, things began to change.

Hauge wrote books on educating children, and creating wealth through righteous businesses. In one place he set up a paper mill, a stamping mill, a bone mill, a flour mill, a tannery, and a foundry. The move of God began to transform the nation. As men were converted they formed co-operatives that set up textile businesses, printing houses and paper mills. New methods of agriculture were promoted.

Believers increasingly affected the areas of society that they moved in. Home, work and social settings were being transformed. Norway eventually became one of the great missionary-sending nations of the world. Cunningham asserts that the wealth and freedom of Norway can be traced back to the movement that began with one man.

The Wesleyan movement in the UK in the 18th century had a significant impact on personal holiness and disciple-making, but it was not until the 19th century that the foundation laid was built into transformational movements. Major advances in children's education, reform of industrial practices, health and welfare innovations were pioneered by Christian men and women. Wilberforce, who was converted in 1785 to an evangelical faith, was probably the greatest of those reformers. He campaigned tirelessly against slavery, until the Abolition of Slavery Act was passed just three days before he died in 1833.

One particularly needy parish in Toxteth, Liverpool, was re-formed as St Nathanial's in 1870. During his thirty years' tenure, Richard Hobson, the vicar, saw the church grow from three people meeting in a cellar to over 3,000 in his newly built parish church and surrounding mission halls. All this was in a parish of only 4,500 people.

As God touched the lives of so many individuals, it changed the whole parish. Formerly a place of many brothels, after fifteen years there were none. While other parishes had illegitimacy rates of up to 65%, in St Nathanial's the rate dropped to 4%. Many abstinence groups paved the way for huge reductions in alcohol consumption and drunkenness.

As a result of the ministry to the poor, the sick list fell to a quarter of its original size. The so-called 'ragged schools' for poor children, allowed many to gain good jobs who otherwise would have had no chance. Hobson made reference to a property owner who employed sixty men, a commercial traveller, a music teacher, a captain of a merchant steamer, and many others who owed their prosperity to the ragged school they had attended.

The Welsh and Hebridean revivals in the 20th century both had transforming impacts on their areas. In both cases pubs closed down as alcohol lost its appeal to the masses, and houses could be left unlocked because of the absence of crime.

Nagaland is an obscure state in North-East India, bordered by China and Bangladesh. Churches were planted there by American Baptist missionaries in the 1800s. When they came, Nagaland was basically a warrior nation, but Christianity reversed the tide of tribal warfare. Through revival movements of the 20th century, the people of Nagaland, formerly animist and Hindu, are now 90% Christian.

This radical transition resulted from a revival that swept through the villages and tribes between 1976 and 1978. Miraculous healings were commonplace as hundreds of people confessed their sins and repented of their old ways. There are proportionately more born-again believers in Nagaland than any other place in the world, according to *Operation World* statistics.

Imagine if every part of your village, town or city was transformed by the presence of Christ

So what can we expect in our towns and cities in the UK? Our starting point is the truth that "everything is possible for him who believes" (Mark 9:23). Let's not assume that these things could never happen here. Why not now? Why not here? Why not through us?

Barring a sovereign move of God that sweeps across our city, we must ask the question, "What will it take?" For the church to have this transformational impact, I believe we need to be the salt, light, and yeast that Jesus called us to be.

What does it mean to be the salt of the earth (Matthew 5:13)? Salt was used in Jesus' day as a preservative and flavouring. It must be scattered to be effective, like that decentralised church model which we looked at earlier. Each of us can be a preserving agent in this corrupt world, calling people to live differently by our example and our words. We must take our place as sons of the kingdom (Matthew 13:38), agents of reconciliation between man and God, and between people (2 Corinthians 5:18-19).

We are also the light of the world (Matthew 5:14). Light is not hidden away but is visible from a distance, illuminating all around it. Jesus prayed that we would be in the world but not of it (John 17:14-18), which means that though we are immersed in our culture, we are distinct from it. It means that we will model something different in our values and lifestyle. Jesus said that we will be misunderstood and even suffer for our faith, so let's not be surprised if we do. But please, let's be persecuted for being like Jesus, not for being religious, hypocritically pious, self-righteous, or just plain weird!

Being light also means modelling something different in social care and education, health and healing, family life and marriage, social enterprises and job creation, and business and wealth creation. The light that is set on a hill may be a project or organisation that challenges received wisdom. A good example is the Christian Fellowship School in Liverpool, contrasting with secular state schools because of its

Christian curriculum and ethos. It is a beacon of light showing that there is another way. It is hugely successful academically, despite a very mixed intake, and the leavers are eagerly accepted for sixth forms at other schools.

The yeast that permeates the whole lump of dough (Matthew 13:33) speaks of the all-pervading influence of the Kingdom of God as we choose to be and do good news wherever God has placed us. We have been sown into the world in anticipation of a harvest of goodness, integrity, innovation, creativity, forgiveness, mercy and kindness. We can change the atmosphere of the places where we live, work and play. We are blessed to be a blessing.

It's time to challenge the way things are done, let the world see what God can do, and what those who are indwelt by the Spirit of God can accomplish.

I applaud the many folk in Frontline who are making a difference where they live and work. Some who are in business are providing jobs, and creating wealth for social projects as well as their companies. Others in the health care professions are giving the extra that love demands to patients and staff who are worried and stressed. Some have taken high levels of responsibility to ensure good services are provided.

Many teachers not only give over and above in the classroom, but also pray for pupils and their families. Deputy heads and head teachers are seeking to make their schools havens of godly peace and security, where the disadvantaged get every opportunity. Others support the community as school governors.

One member of the Frontline family said this about her involvement in her children's school as a governor: "When my children started at their local primary school there was no PTFA (Parents, Teachers and Friends Association). I started to volunteer in school, and then set about re-establishing the group. Research shows that where parents are involved in the school their child attends, that child is likely to do better. In our school, many families have no one in employment, and motivation to engage in education can be low.

"Last year the new PTFA ran its first Christmas Fair. We worked together as a team and carried each other's burdens. More parents got involved and despite the economic downturn we raised more money than before. James 3:18 says that those who sow in peace will raise a harvest of righteousness. Handling conflict without blowing up at people is high on my agenda, and in several situations anger has been dispersed and grace has been found. A group of Christian parents have prayed for the PTFA and been the backbone of all that I've been able to do.

"Our successes have been hard won, with sleepless nights and struggles for direction, and our PTFA faces an on-going fight for survival, but we're getting there. I have the privilege of working with some amazing parents, and it's very humbling as we share our strengths and weaknesses. It's been hard to keep going when criticism comes, but as long as I keep my eyes fixed on serving God and being faithful to his calling, I get through it."

I believe in the power of one and in the power of all

Praise God for frontline troops, parents and teachers who seek to bless our schools in this way.

We can all contribute to transforming our city, and we must. It will not happen without every member playing their part. Some say it takes just five percent of a population to change something fundamental in the culture or way of life. The church has run many projects over the years, including a soup kitchen, an after-school homework club, bingo for the elderly, a parent and toddler group, and an outreach to local children and their families called Kidz Klub.

The Kidz Klub has had a massive influence on thousands of children throughout the city: teachers talk about how children have changed and parents see the change too. The weekly visits have been a lifeline for some families who just need someone to talk to. Seventeen years of Kidz Klub means a whole generation has been influenced. A youth mentoring project has grown out of it and now helps steer the lives of many young people away from crime, towards productive employment and responsible relationships.

CAP (Christians Against Poverty)[2] have been working with those in crippling debt for many years. One CAP client recently said how her whole life had been changed by the help she had received. On top of getting right out of debt in two years, she was also reconciled with her parents and is now seeing God work in her children's lives.

Another client said, "Since CAP helped me, life has changed in a big way. I used to be overwhelmed with stress, waking up through the night worrying about all the bills I couldn't pay. I was behind with water and council tax, and every day I got two or three phone calls about the money I owed. I felt completely hopeless and couldn't see a way out.

"Within a few weeks of contacting the CAP Centre at Frontline, they stopped the creditors phoning up all the time and took the letters away, which was a huge relief. Claire (the centre manager) came and helped me work out a budget I could stick to each week, so I always knew I would have enough money to buy food and essentials. Then, all I had to do was pay a set amount each week into a new CAP account for my bills and debt.

"Now my whole life is different! I'm back into work, I'm not stressed anymore, I'm spending my money more wisely and I feel like a new person. I've had a real boost in energy and am living a healthier lifestyle now. I've even had compliments from friends who've noticed how much chirpier I am. I honestly reckon I would have hanged myself without CAP's help – and now look at me."

Inform, a project working with women struggling with a crisis pregnancy or post-abortion trauma, have seen many women helped to make informed decisions about their pregnancy, and others to be truly healed of the pain of their abortion.

Streetwise, working with street sex-workers, has befriended many of the girls who put their lives at risk through street sex in order to pay for their drug habit. Coffee, sandwiches, and a chat make all the difference. One or two have been supported to come out of that lifestyle.

One of the girls said, "When you first met me years ago, we were living in a squat or on the streets and life was rubbish. Things are loads better now. Part of that was through friends on Streetwise sticking by us, like Jude who even came with me when I had to go to court. We're slowly getting off the drugs, but you need people to believe you can do it."

I believe that the church can bring transformation to the city

So whether it's a taxi driver going the extra mile to help a passenger, a mum supporting a struggling single parent in her street, an employer giving his staff the best training and support to help develop them, an office worker praying for her boss and colleagues to be blessed, or a journalist trying to expose injustice, we all play our part in seeing our city being transformed.

Imagine if even five percent of the population of your town or city lived and worked to be divine salt, light, and yeast

Imagine if every church ran projects and services to bless their communities. Imagine if every church cooperated with other churches to have a coordinated impact on the neighbourhood. Imagine if those in positions of influence used them to bring God's kingdom agenda to bear in our city, making policy and shaping culture. Imagine!

Questions for discussion:

- Explain why the gospel is transformational.

- Where can you play your part in this agenda?

- In what way are we waiting for God to act, and in what ways is God waiting for us to act?

Endnotes

1. Cunningham, L. and Rogers, J., *The Book that Transforms Nations: The Power of the Bible to Change Any Country*, (YWAM Publishing, 2007)

2. www.capuk.org

12. Where is it all going?

Steven Covey in his best-selling book *Seven Habits of Highly Effective People*[1] talks about the principle of "starting with the end in mind." This is a good principle for life. If we want to end up somewhere in particular, we need to understand not only where we are, but where we are headed, and make our plans for today and tomorrow with that destination in mind.

For the Christian there is one clear destination. The early church referred to it as their great hope: the hope of eternity spent with Father, Son and Holy Spirit, of ruling and reigning with him in the new heavens and new earth (Revelation 5:10). When it comes to our mission on earth, it's important that we keep the end in mind.

The Father created us with the longing for a great family, "a people belonging to God" (1 Peter 2:9). As we draw closer to the time of Christ's return and look at the numbers of people who are turning to

Christ across the world today, it must bring joy to his heart. It has been said that there are more Christians alive today than in the last 2,000 years all put together. No wonder he has waited all this time to send Jesus back for his bride. The best is clearly yet to come.

But many believe that there will be an end-time generation that will see the greatest outpouring of God's Spirit, the greatest ingathering of souls, and the appearing of the most magnificent bride, the church of Jesus Christ, in preparation for the bridegroom's return.

What are the conditions for his return, and why has he delayed coming? It seems clear that the early church expected him to come back in their lifetime. In 2 Peter 3:9, Peter says that the Lord is patient, and doesn't want any to perish, but for all to come to repentance. He goes on to say that we can play our part to "speed the coming" of the "day of God," that is, by working to complete our mission (2 Peter 3:12).

When talking to his disciples about the end of this age, Jesus says, "And this gospel of the kingdom will be preached in the whole world as a testimony to all nations [or *peoples*], and then the end will come" (Matthew 24:14). We are getting close to the target of reaching every nation, but there are still unreached people groups. Some say the task could be completed within a decade.

Will we be the generation to complete it? There is no reason why not. We have the resources, we have the man and womanpower, we have the technology; we just need the will.

In Revelation John the writer speaks of the marriage of the Lamb and the moment of Christ's return, saying, "and his bride has made herself ready" (Revelation 19:7). One aspect of this readiness is having completed the mission so burning on the Father's heart – that all men, women and children should receive an invitation to the wedding (Matthew 22:2-10). That every person hears, understands, and has the opportunity to respond to the gospel (1 Timothy 2:4).

But another condition of the Lord's return is seen in Ephesians. Paul says that Christ is at work sanctifying the church, bringing it to maturity. He says, "Christ loved the church and gave himself up for her to make her holy, cleansing her by the washing with water through the word, and to present her to himself as a radiant church, without stain or wrinkle or any other blemish, but holy and blameless" (Ephesians 5:25-27).

We are being made holy, that is, set apart for him, pure in heart and conduct. We know that we will not be perfect until he comes and our old sinful nature is finally done away with, but we are called to maturity. I believe we will be a united, healed, fully functioning church that is passionate about Jesus, a church where the members are knit together and playing to each other's strengths, a church that is committed to reaching out to the least, the last, and the lost.

It's a church that is no longer arguing about what colour the carpet should be, but has understood its amazing significance in God's plan for planet Earth. It knows that the church is God's "A Plan," and that there is no "Plan B."

So it's both quantity and quality – the greatest number possible of people in heaven, and the highest degree of maturity and purity. What a church that will be. It's the church I have given myself to discover and be a part of since I was nineteen. I hope you will join me on the quest to grow this church, to invest in this church, to see this church be all that Jesus died for. As the early Moravian missionaries sailed off to unknown lands and great danger, they said it was so "that the Lamb that was slain might receive the reward of his suffering."

Finally, that great day will come when the greatest "sound and light" show in the heavens will begin. The sun and moon will be supernaturally darkened as Jesus the Lord of Glory appears in the skies, displaying the splendour of his majesty and brilliance. Everyone will see him.

Imagine if the church was so passionate that every people group was reached with the gospel

Imagine it: there will be the sound of the trumpet of God, the voice of the archangel, and the shout of the Lord – yes, imagine (Matthew 24:27-31, 1 Thessalonians 4:16). That electrifying shout will shake the heavens like an earthquake shakes the earth. It will be terrifying for those who have rejected Christ and are perishing, and awesome for those who know his voice. It will be like the roar of Aslan in *The Lion, the Witch and the Wardrobe*[2], both frightening and reassuring.

I believe that Jesus will come back for a wonderful church that has reached its full potential

Then the angels will go to the four corners of the earth and gather all the saints, those made right with God through the blood of Jesus, to be with him in the air (Matthew 24:31, 1 Thessalonians 4:17). It is the only gathering place big enough for the welcoming party for the Lord of lords. The kingdom will be completed and the devil and wicked will be judged (Revelation 20:10-15). The marriage feast will begin (Matthew 22:1-14 and 26:29, Revelation 19:7-9).

Creation will be liberated from its bondage to decay and destruction, imposed by the fall. Natural disasters and environmental damage will no longer afflict us, and all believers will receive their resurrection bodies (Romans 8:18-24). The new heavens and the new earth will be revealed and the bride and groom will descend to take their rightful place on the earth to rule and reign for ever (Revelation 5:10). The church is also described as a city. This city, the new Jerusalem, will appear coming down out of heaven (Revelation 21:2). There will be no sun or moon now, as the glory of the Lord illuminates this city (Revelation 21:23). And we will be with him forever. Amen!

What a glorious day. A day worth being ready for.

So where are you now?

As well as knowing where you are going, it's also important to know where you are. It's fundamental to all navigation. When you are plotting a course with sat nav, it will ask you for your current location. So where are you? It's the question that the Lord called out to Adam when he was lost in the Garden of Eden after he had sinned against the Lord, "Where are you?" (Genesis 3:9). The same question rings out across the millennia and reaches our hearts today. Are you passive and coasting? Are you bored and disconnected? Are you offended and isolated? Are you disillusioned and cynical? Or are you passionate and connected, making your best contribution? Where do you think the Lord wants you to be?

We all need a helping hand from time to time, but we are still responsible for our own lives. When we meet the Lord, it will be no use blaming others, as Adam blamed Eve, or blaming Satan, as Eve did (Genesis 3:12-13). We alone are responsible for mastering the things that threaten to knock us off course or disqualify us. The Lord says to us as he did to Cain, "Sin is crouching at the door; it desires to have you, but you must master it" (Genesis 4:7).

We need to decide whether we will play safe or live dangerously. Will we abandon all attempts to live for ourselves and live to please him? Will we get over our discontent, disillusionment, and offence, and reconnect with God's people so we can play our part in this amazing thing called the church? Will we believe in all that she can be, and help the church become the bride that Jesus died for and is coming back for? I believe there is nothing comparable worth living for.

Imagine if the church was so pure and mature that it was ready for the return of the Bridegroom

This magnificent obsession has filled most of my waking and many of my sleeping hours for the last 38 years. There have been many disappointments and setbacks. The pace of change has been slower than I had hoped. Many would have disqualified me along the way. But the Father believes in me. He loves me and has called me to challenge others to 'be the church'.

He believes in you. He sees your amazing potential. He sees the unique gifts and qualities that he gave you. He sees you finding joy among his people. He sees you making an incredible contribution. He sees you investing your treasure in heaven and reaping an eternal reward.

Let's do it; let's be the church!

This is my manifesto.

Nic Harding

Endnotes

1. Covey, S. R., *The Seven Habits of Highly Effective People: Powerful Lessons in Personal Change*, (Free Press, 1989)

2. Lewis, C.S., *The Lion, the Witch and the Wardrobe*, (Geoffrey Bles, 1950)